"If you want to be challenged to a more intentional and purposeful prayer life, read and digest this book! *Strategic Prayer* applies warfare principles to the spiritual war in which we are engaged and provides practical keys for more effective intercession whether applied to an individual person or an entire people. An excellent resource to add to your prayer arsenal!"

    —Jane Hansen
       President/CEO Aglow International

Books by

Eddie Smith

FROM BETHANY HOUSE PUBLISHERS

EDDIE SMITH
MICHAEL L. HENNEN

STRATEGIC PRAYER

APPLYING THE POWER | *of* | TARGETED PRAYER

BETHANYHOUSE
MINNEAPOLIS, MINNESOTA

Strategic Prayer
Copyright © 2007
Eddie Smith and Michael L. Hennen

Cover design by Lookout Design, Inc.

Page 192 is a continuation of the copyright page.

Published by Bethany House Publishers
11400 Hampshire Avenue South
Bloomington, Minnesota 55438

Bethany House Publishers is a division of
Baker Publishing Group,
Grand Rapids, Michigan.

Printed in the United States of America

ISBN-13: 978-0-7642-0342-8
ISBN-10: 0-7642-0342-8

Library of Congress Cataloging-in-Publication Data

Smith, Eddie.
    Strategic prayer : applying the power of targeted prayer / Eddie Smith, Michael L. Hennen.
        p. cm.
        Summary: "This book is primarily for intercessors and church leaders who want to become more effective in praying for their community and nation. Time-tested principles and strategies from two authors with experience in the field of prayer"—Provided by publisher.
        ISBN-13: 978-0-7642-0342-8 (pbk.)
        ISBN-10: 0-7642-0342-8 (pbk.)
        1. Intercessory prayer—Christianity. 2. Spiritual warfare. I. Hennen, Michael L. II. Title.
        BV210.3.S65   2007
        248.3'2—dc22   2006038327

We dedicate this book to "people of prayer," God's intercessors, who demonstrate the heart of God for the nations and whose abandonment to His purposes in the earth continues to challenge us.

E D D I E   S M I T H , the cofounder and president of the U.S. Prayer Center, is a cross-denominational prayer leader and teacher, an internationally known conference speaker, and an author. Before founding the U.S. Prayer Center in 1990, Eddie and his wife, Alice, served sixteen years in itinerant evangelism and fourteen years in local churches. Eddie and Alice make their home in Houston, Texas.

M I C H A E L   H E N N E N has served as a pastor, a missionary to diverse cultures and people, and a church planter with the Global 12 Project. Michael coordinates the internship program of Gateways Beyond International, a Messianic discipleship training school, and partners with Joyce Meyer Ministries as an administrator for programming and follow-up. Michael and his wife, Aimee, spend most of their time in the Middle East and return periodically to Baton Rouge, Louisiana.

⟩(CONTENTS)⟨

PART 3 : THE BATTLEGROUND OF THE MIND

PART 4 : PROACTIVE PRAYER

INTRODUCTION

EDDIE'S INTRODUCTION

---

stra • te • gic also stra • te • gi • cal *adj.*

1. Of or relating to strategy. **2.a.** Important or essential in relation to a plan of action. **b.** Essential to the effective conduct of war. **c.** Highly important to an intended objective. **3.** Intended to destroy the military potential of an enemy. stra • te • gi • cal • ly *adv.*

Without question, prayer is the most important—and potentially the most powerful—tool in a Christian's arsenal. And do I need to inform or remind you that all of us were born into a war and live on a battlefield?

The conflict between the forces of good and evil, of God and Satan, has been raging since the day sin was found in Satan's heart (see Isaiah 14). We're in the fight, and prayer is our primary weapon.

Strategic prayer, in connection with the above definition of *strategic*, is essential prayer that is necessary to conduct war, accomplish an objective, and destroy the enemy and his devices.

The problem is, much of our praying is pointless, passionless, and powerless. It's poorly formed, thoughtlessly presented, and we wonder why it's largely ineffective.

I'm such a pragmatist that I'm irritated at the way many of us pray without preparation and, worst of all, without expectation! We keep looking for problems to fire off in prayer for God's attention but then pay no attention at all to His response. We can list ten prayer requests but couldn't begin to report ten things God has done in reply. *We're actually ignoring God in our prayers.*

It's time we learn to pray practical, specific, result-oriented prayers. After all, the earth is our Lord's, the fullness of it, and everyone who lives on it. He's filling it with the knowledge of His glory! (Psalm 24:1; Habakkuk 2:14). And He's invited *us* into a joint-venture partnership with Him to complete it.

My wife, Alice, is one who was called at an early age to pray for the nations. I've watched her develop in her calling. I've learned from her. She is passionate about the King and His kingdom, radical in her allegiance to Him. But unlike so many dedicated intercessors, she is realistic and sensible about her intercessory ministry. She refuses to move presumptuously. She never hesitates to admit when she's missed the target. She holds herself and any team with whom she prays to the highest standards. I gladly admit that much of what I share in this book is a result of her intercessory labor.

Michael Hennen, my coauthor, is amazing. Young enough to be my son and wise enough to be my father, Michael is an "anointed genius." The perceptions he shares in this book are invaluable to those seriously involved in praying for territory and to those wanting useful teaching and instruction. He's not a theorist, he's a practitioner. He proves his theories. He and his wife, Aimee, are serving the Lord in some of the hardest and most dangerous places on earth. It's my privilege to partner with him in this work.

I pray that Father God will open your eyes to the immense potential of your smallest prayer.

Blessings,
Eddie Smith

MICHAEL'S INTRODUCTION

The enemy is real, and his designs are carefully planned. If we want to be more effective against him, we need to understand the strategies he uses and the objectives on which those strategies are focused.

There are concrete reasons for every form of demonic oppression, whether personal, communal, or national. Our prayer-effectiveness in these realms will be severely limited until we discover the enemy's goals. The world today suffers from extensive demonic terrorism. Until we clearly comprehend the devil's motives, strategies, and goals, the question of how to combat that terrorism will remain a mystery.

This book addresses the practical need to identify and prioritize prayer targets. Its principles reflect a theology born more out of life experience than the classroom. While living in the former Soviet Union, I became aware of certain strategies the government utilized to aid the spread and entrenchment of communism. This commune-"ism" yielded widespread social oppression and carried out an effective global assault on peoples and cultures.

"Isms" are generally spirit-inspired strategies formulated to overrun and control society. Behind each "ism" is a ruling spirit. By identifying the principles employed by these spirits, we can identify demonic priorities. These priorities reflect front-line areas where the spiritual battle rages most fiercely. It is here that the devil risks the most and stands most to gain or to lose.

METHODS AND PRINCIPLES

Methods don't always work, but principles do. The effectiveness of spiritual methods depends largely on the conditions of the spiritual environment and the experience of those employing them. Attention to spiritual principles, regardless of environment or experience, always brings positive results.

Part One, "Warring in Spiritual Realms," is based on principles employed by the Soviet Union to launch an effective military coup. We use this analogy because the devil has deployed his forces to launch a spiritual coup against God. Though we already know the outcome of this attempt, knowledge of the devil's goals and strategies will help us to vanquish him more quickly.

Part Two, "Spiritual Strategy," identifies specific spiritual strategies that the forces of good or evil may employ to launch a successful offensive.

Part Three, "The Battleground of the Mind," focuses on how to prepare the mind for victory.

Part Four, "Proactive Prayer," suggests how we may pray proactively by taking an active, offensive stance against enemy strongholds. The gates of hell (defensive) shall not prevail against the church (offensive), and the body of Christ will plunder the treasures of darkness (Matthew 16:18; Isaiah 45:1–3).

Finally, as its title implies, the overriding purpose of *Strategic Prayer* is to equip you to pray more strategically. Accordingly, at the end of each section, we've placed questions that will focus your attention on the corporate and personal application of each principle.

PROCESS VERSUS PERSON

"There is no power in prayer!" This shocking revelation, first expressed to me by my wife, is one most of us have yet to discover. *Our faith is not in a process—it's in a Person.* The power of our prayers is resident in the person of God, and our effectiveness as intercessors is wholly dependent on the quality of our relationship with Him. That quality is best expressed through faith.

What do we believe about God's power and character? Our faith is an expression of our intimacy with Him. If we truly know Him, we pray according to His will and are fully convinced of the integrity of His character that always accomplishes His Word.

The only power of prayer is in our understanding of and submission to God's authority. Effective prayer is faithfully aligning oneself under His authority to speak and to do His Word and will. It is not the process that wields power in prayer but the Person who empowers prayer for His own purposes.

We have written this book to magnify a Person. Our desire is to direct those with a pure heart for God toward greater discernment and greater understanding of truly effective intercession. *Strategic Prayer* is not a replacement for the intimacy with God that will make you a truly effective intercessor. It is a prayer reconnaissance manual.

Rich blessings,
Michael Hennen

AUTHORS' SUGGESTIONS

To pray more strategically, it's always helpful to take a spiritual survey of your circumstances. Answering the questions that follow each section will help you draw a spiritual map of circumstances and will focus your attention on the personal and corporate application of each strategic prayer principle.

Don't hurry. Completing the survey is not the objective. But don't skip over it. Our goal is to help you discover the truth about your circumstances that will give you the fullest perspective and equip you most powerfully to change them. The only wrong answers are those contrived to impress others. The only right answers are those led by the Spirit of Truth.

When you and others in your group have finished your surveys, compare notes to see if there's a consensus. Perhaps such comparison will illuminate strongholds and priorities that deserve more corporate or personal attention. If you're the group leader, submit your observations to your pastor for consideration. Wait for the Spirit's leading, through those who cover you, before proceeding with any strategic and corporate prayer initiatives.

Even if you take the survey more for personal than for corporate reasons, it's still a good idea to pray with others regarding the life issues you're facing. For prayer, seek those who know you well and whose lives exhibit Christ's compassion and character. They may be family members, home-group or cell-group leaders, or other friends or leaders in the church. As you pray together in agreement, we trust and pray that increased freedom and authority in prayer will emerge and that you'll discover a greater intimacy with the Lord.

PART 1 WARRING IN
SPIRITUAL
REALMS

STRATEGIC AND TACTICAL PRAYER

PRAYER MUST PROCEED SIMULTANEOUSLY ON
BOTH A STRATEGIC AND A TACTICAL TRACK
TOWARD A DEFINITE DESTINATION.

There are 1,200–1,500 demolition companies worldwide that raze skyscrapers, chimneys, towers, bridges, and other structures. At least two things set Baltimore, Maryland-based Controlled Demolition, Inc. (CDI) apart.

First, CDI, founded in 1960 by Jack Loizeaux (retired in 1984), today is a family business run by his two sons, Marc and Doug, and Marc's daughter Stacey.

Second, CDI is the globe's undisputed champion of large-structure implosions. Whether a 2,000-ton skyscraper, a 384-foot communications tower, or the Seattle Kingdome—by volume the largest building ever demolished by explosives—they will bring it down. CDI holds four Guinness Book world records and has imploded more than 7,000 structures—more than all their competitors combined!

Their projects are amazing to witness. In mere seconds massive edifices crumble in on themselves in a shower of dust and debris. Perhaps the very essence of Controlled Demolition's work is in their name: CONTROL.

Each project CDI accepts requires months of precision planning by a world-renowned team of engineering experts to determine the best equipment, materials, manpower, and methods to be used. Their goal? Guaranteed complete predictability.

While being interviewed for a Learning Channel special on CDI, President Marc Loizeaux was asked, "How do you determine how much explosive will be required to bring down a large structure?" He replied, "The secret isn't in knowing how much explosive to use; the secret is in knowing where to place it."

Engineers determine exactly which steel beam must be severed with explosives, what concrete masses must be pulverized, and in what sequence everything should happen. The building is then rigged with timed explosives. On the day of the implosion, one pressed button releases a chain reaction of explosions; the structure that required years to build collapses in seconds.

One day when I (Eddie) returned home from a speaking engagement, I was stunned to see that the beautiful four-bedroom home at the end of our block had burned to the ground. As I stood looking at the charred remains the Lord spoke to my heart. He pointed out that while more than nine months went into building the house, it was destroyed in less than ninety minutes.

Then He said, "Satan is angry about what the church is learning today about strategic prayer. He is angry because he has but a short time" (see Revelation 12:12). It has taken Satan thousands of years to construct his demonic network for promoting evil around the world. *What targeted, strategic prayer can destroy in a few minutes, Satan has neither time nor resources left to rebuild.*

STRATEGY AND TACTICS

As Marc Loizeaux explained, what's critical in demolishing man-made structures is knowing where to put each explosive and in what order to detonate them. As for spiritual structures, one of the biggest challenges facing any intentional intercessor is knowing how to prioritize prayer. We're surrounded by pressing needs, so many expressions of satanic activity in our lives, our homes, our cities, our nations; *how do we know where and how to invest prayer?* And how can we be certain that our prayer coverage is adequate? The answer to these questions is *prayer targeting.* In the same way the military carefully evaluates and selects its target objectives, so must we carefully evaluate and select ours.

STRATEGIC PRAYER TARGETING

We use *strategic prayer targeting* to prioritize our prayer to achieve a specific goal.

First we define our goal: What do we hope to accomplish through prayer? If we don't know our goal, we won't know how to pray. Our goal ought to be well-defined, specific, and comprehensive; if it's vague, indefinite, or incomplete, our prayers will certainly fall short of their mark.

Hebrews 11 offers what some call the Hall of Faith, a list of the faithful throughout biblical history; then it makes a startling declaration:

> These all died in faith, not having received the promises, but having seen them afar off, and were persuaded of them, and embraced them. (v. 13 KJV)

When prayer groups or praying individuals "run out of steam" (lose faith), it's usually because their prayers were vague, indefinite, or incomplete; they've not seen, been persuaded of, or embraced their goal.

Once we have a clearly defined, nonnegotiable, ample goal, we can prioritize our prayers: we know where to put the explosive (where to direct our prayer, the target). Now we need to prioritize our detonations, that is, the order in which we detonate (pray our prayers) to accomplish the goal.

How do we prioritize our prayers?

We prioritize our prayers along two parallel, complementary tracks: tactical and strategic. Consider your prayer as a locomotive traveling down rails that lead to your specified target or goal (your defined destination).

▸ *Strategic prayers target the enemy* (powers and principalities).

▸ *Tactical prayers focus on the subjects* acted against by the enemy (powers and principalities) (see Ephesians 6:12).

For example, praying against a spirit of communism is a strategic prayer. Praying for people influenced by the spirit of communism is a tactical prayer. If we fail to pray against principalities and powers, their ability to influence people will not diminish. If we fail to pray for the people, their tendency to yield to powers and principalities will only increase.

MISSION-CRITICAL INFORMATION

How do we know, at any given time, whether the tactical target or the strategic target is more urgent? In both physical and spiritual warfare, *strategic timing* is "mission-critical information." A prayer prayed at the wrong time is the wrong prayer. If our targeting process isn't sufficiently flexible to accommodate changes in circumstances, then our prayers will miss the mark when the circumstances change. To properly prioritize prayer, we must apply flexible targeting techniques. Flexible targeting techniques depend on reliable reconnaissance (investigation).

Reliable reconnaissance makes prayer strategic. *Strategic timing makes reconnaissance reliable, and strategic timing is the exclusive competence of the Holy Spirit.*

Intelligent targeting requires vigilant reconnaissance. We must engage in thorough research and become well informed of circumstances in natural and spiritual realms. Spiritual mapping often provides much-needed detail for effective prayer. We should neither neglect to map the influence of evil powers over nations nor ignore their current influence over the lives of people.

Nevertheless, the most critical reconnaissance relies more on the Spirit's direction than on our efforts. Without it, all forms of reconnaissance will amount to little more than spiritual vanity. With it, our vigilance can and does discover truly mission-critical information: the right knowledge in the right place at the right time.

MAPPING: TWO KINDS

George Otis Jr. has defined spiritual mapping, our reconnaissance of the spiritual world, as "superimposing our understanding of forces and events in the spiritual domain onto places and circumstances in the material world" (*Last of the Giants*, 85). Spiritual mapping identifies and defines the geographic or cultural pattern of spiritual oppression.

Its counterpart in the natural world is cultural mapping: defining the sociological patterns of common traditions practiced among one or more distinct people groups. These traditions, practiced by people, are the rituals through which spiritual forces establish a stronghold within a culture.

Spiritual mapping is *strategic* (relating to principalities and powers). Cultural mapping is *tactical* (relating to the people the enemy is affecting). They are complementary, and they're of equal value in forming an effective prayer strategy and in selecting prayer targets.

When we lay our understanding of forces and events in the spiritual domain over our outline of cultural traditions, we can clearly see what our strategic and tactical prayer priorities must be.

KEY POINTS

(1) Clearly define your strategic and tactical prayer goals.
   (a) Strategic prayers target powers and principalities.
   (b) Tactical prayers target those whom powers and principalities act against.
(2) Your prayer goal must be well-defined, specific, and comprehensive.
(3) Prioritize your prayers along the parallel and complementary tracks of strategic and tactical prayer.
(4) Reliable reconnaissance makes prayer strategic.
(5) The Holy Spirit (not our efforts) leads us to the right place at the right time and opens our eyes to truly mission-critical information.
(6) Traditions are the rituals through which spiritual forces establish cultural strongholds.

SPIRITUAL RECONNAISSANCE

(1) What prevailing demonic powers and principalities are exercising influence over our territory?
(2) Which of these can be identified as the ruling spirit?
(3) Who are the people against whom these powers and principalities act, and who are their leaders?
(4) What appear to be the Holy Spirit's current mission-critical prayer priorities in this territory?
(5) What cultural rituals serve to deeply imbed the influence of these powers and principalities in the people's hearts and minds?

PERSONALIZE IT

(1) What demonic powers and principalities are exercising influence in my life?

(2) Can one of these be identified as the dominant source of spiritual attack?

(3) How do I discern when these powers and principalities are active against me, and through what relationships or situations do they tend to act?

(4) What appears to be the Holy Spirit's most mission-critical prayer priority for my personal life at this time?

(5) What personal habits, traditions, or rituals serve to deeply imbed the influence of oppressive powers and principalities in my heart and mind?

TARGETING THE POWER GRID

IF THE POWER GRID IS DESTABILIZED,

ALL ELEMENTS THAT DEPEND ON IT

WILL ALSO BECOME UNSTABLE.

I n the summer of 1994, while serving as a missionary in Russia, I (Michael) was asked by a television crew for an interview. One of my friends suggested that it would be great publicity for our new church, so reluctantly, ignoring the check in my spirit, I agreed. Our church, I reasoned, had already suffered so much at the media's hands. It was time to turn the tide. Besides, we represented just one of many faiths that would be profiled in the coming weeks. Should we remain silent and let the cults get all the attention?

I waited patiently for the day of the interview, which finally took place in my living room. Then I waited more patiently to see it aired on the local station. During the interview I had been discomfited by the crew's strange questions, but I did my best to accent the importance of a personal relationship with Christ while also responding to inquiries about the book of Revelation and "the mark of the beast."

———————

When our visa ran out, we had to leave the country to get it renewed. Upon returning, we were told that the interview had done more harm than good—because of it some had even left the church. When I asked our members about the negative results, I was told that in the interview I had argued with a Russian Orthodox priest.

I was dumbfounded. I'd never even met a Russian Orthodox priest! But my church members insisted: "You were arguing with him right there in your living room. We saw it on TV. We recognized the wallpaper."

To this day, I do not know how it was done. Obviously it involved some intricate editing, but I'd been thoroughly duped. The montage was so effective that even my own members insisted on what they had seen. From that day, I banned all recorders and video cameras from the church and never again agreed to another interview. I decided that God doesn't need publicity!

———————

For six years the KGB tracked me, and they always knew when I was leaving the country. On one occasion they sent an agent the day before my wife and I left for America. I knew they knew when I would leave; they knew that I knew and never hid the fact that they were KGB. I had nothing to hide, which was good because they seemed to know everything anyway. What really irked me is that while I was entirely honest, they were deceptive. I was willing to die to tell the truth, while they were willing to do almost anything to stop me. Why? What did they have to hide?

In natural warfare, strategic targets are those that provide communication, transportation, leadership, and supplies to a military force. In successful spiritual warfare, to select the right prayer targets and form effective prayer strategies, we must identify the spiritual counterparts of these targets.

In the natural realm, such targets are fueled by what's called the power grid. If the power grid (electricity and other forms of fuel and energy) is destabilized, every element that depends on it will also become unstable. When fuel and energy stop flowing, communication and transportation slow down. The production of supplies stops, and leadership fails.

THE DEVIL'S POWER GRID

The devil's power grid is *deception*. All his works are fueled by lies. He cannot afford to broadcast truth and must resist its proliferation at all costs. The truth always assails his power grid and neutralizes his efforts. The devil resists truth by spreading *lies!*

Through what communication media does he do this? For one thing, he broadcasts through the words of unrighteous leaders. When these leaders ally with one another for the sake of convenience, they form a demonic communication network. This network doesn't depend as much on high technology as on low morals.

The only way to destabilize the devil's deceptive power grid is with the truth. *The answer to the devil's aggression is not the absence of lies but the proclamation of truth.* Only in the light of truth will the proliferation of wickedness cease and man's commerce with the devil diminish. Only the light of truth can displace the deception that darkens the minds of men. So in the process of choosing prayer targets, truth's proliferation must be preeminent.

TRUTH IS VIOLENT

Where the lies of the devil stop flowing, the illusory nature of his power is revealed and his influence dissolves. People who've never heard the truth have no alternative but to believe a lie. The devil's influence over such people remains until the truth is revealed and accepted.

In our battle against deception, *the best defense is a good offense.* We must take the initiative not only to resist the demonic advance but also to advance against the gates of hell with the truth. As the devil vomits forth his foul river of lies, the kingdom of God suffers violence, but the violent shall take it by force (Matthew 11:12). The truth is violent! Its confrontational nature exposes wickedness. Those who love darkness hate truth. But the gates of hell shall not prevail against us.

GOD'S POWER GRID

God's power grid is *truth.* With God's truth we expose the deeds of darkness and conquer fear and bondage. God's Word is *truth* (Psalm 119:160). If we abide in His Word, we are His disciples, and we shall know the *truth* and the *truth* shall make us free (John 8:31–32). "God is spirit, and those who worship Him must worship in spirit and *truth*" (4:24). (All emphasis in Scriptures throughout the book has been added.) Jesus is the way, the *truth*, and the life (14:6), and no one comes to the Father except through Him.

This is the *truth* that frees people from the devil's bondage. We must speak this *truth* in love, "that we should no longer be children, tossed to and fro and carried about with every wind of doctrine, by the trickery of men, in the cunning craftiness of deceitful plotting, but, speaking the truth in love, may grow up in all things into Him who is the head; Christ" (Ephesians 4:14–15 NKJV). *Truth*, God's power grid, is a smart bomb against the devil's power grid!

APPLICATION

KEY POINTS

(1) When the power grid is destabilized, leadership fails.

(2) Deception is the devil's power grid.

(3) All the devil's works are empowered by lies.

(4) Satan cannot afford to broadcast truth and must resist its proliferation.

(5) The devil communicates his lies through the words of unrighteous leaders.

(6) Truth destabilizes the devil's deceptive power grid.

(7) A person who's never heard the truth has no alternative but to believe a lie.

(8) Truth is God's power grid.

SPIRITUAL RECONNAISSANCE

(1) What are three predominant cultural lies that seem to hold the people of our region in bondage?

(2) What is God's scriptural antidote to these lies?

(3) What is Satan's predominant method for spreading these lies in our culture?

PERSONALIZE IT

(1) What are three predominant lies of my worldview that seem to hold me in bondage?

(2) What is God's scriptural antidote to these lies?

(3) What is Satan's predominant method for spreading these lies in my life?

▸((3))◂

TARGETING COMMUNICATION

EVERY WAR IS AN INFORMATION WAR.

Every war is an information war. In conflict, conclusions drawn are based on the flow and availability of information and on the filters used to select and interpret that information. Americans have seen this in the Iraq war and on the question of weapons of mass destruction.

Those who regulate the flow of information can virtually dictate the warfare's direction, duration, and intensity. The communication of information mobilizes forces to act. The regulation of communication holds the greatest long-term threat to an opposing force. Thus, it's in the best interest of governments, natural and spiritual, to govern the flow of information toward meeting their own ends.

This governing of information flow depends heavily on how people select and interpret information. Its selection and interpretation is most effectively governed by creating worldview filters that filter out opposing views. These are created through propaganda. Propaganda is perpetrated by those who, in one sense, become transmission towers for their government—natural or spiritual.

PROPAGANDA

One of the first rights to vanish under a repressive government is the right to a free press. This is also one of the first rights to be restored by an emerging government with nothing to hide or fear. The devil loves to control the press but loathes the press that opposes him. As long as he controls the press he will continue, unhindered, to spread his propaganda. And he will continue to control the press as long as people let him.

People listen to what they want to hear. The devil knows what lies people love most and will happily broadcast them to stroke egos. Communication is a two-way process: Satan is lying, and the hearer is willing to listen to his lies. What makes propaganda effective is people's willingness to accept unsubstantiated information. People listen to lies for at least four reasons:

(1) Because they are given no clear alternative
(2) Because it's more convenient to believe the lie than the truth
(3) Because the devil has distorted the truth enough to make it false but not enough to make it distasteful
(4) Because the lie is so fantastically blatant that, in our naïveté, we cannot imagine it could be false.

TRUTH

The first is relatively easy to resolve. Where there is no alternative to deception, we should provide one. We can engage the devil's lies with the truth of our testimony and with the weapon of God's Word. Without an alternative, a person has no choice but to believe a lie. A person presented with an alternative—truth—has a choice.

TACTICAL PRAYER

The second problem, when falsehood is more convenient than truth, is not so easily resolved. This requires tactical prayer on behalf of the deceived individual whose mind is becoming reprobate. The person is not only deceived but willfully so. Truth won't provide the whole antidote; the person is willfully in bondage to the lusts of this world. He cannot accept the truth until convenience is dethroned. Tactical prayer is essential to his spiritual freedom.

STRATEGIC PRAYER

The third problem, falsehood that isn't distasteful, also requires tactical prayer. However, because it involves malicious propagation of deception, it also requires strategic prayer. This individual, the victim, has a spirit blinding his mind. That spirit must be bound and the deception being used as a weapon against him must be exposed and destroyed.

Communism, founded on distortions of Christian principles, is a perfect example of such a demonic tactic. A person's mind must be freed from this deception *and* the spiritual principality that propagates it must be bound.

SPIRITUAL WARFARE PRAYER

The fourth problem, the fantastically blatant deception, is by far the most difficult. Atheism and macroevolution are blatant examples. Those who believe there is no God will not accept any evidence that verifies His existence. They remain bound in their reasoning that "since there is no God, all evidence pointing to His existence must be false." Breaking this level of bondage will also require tactical and strategic prayer. Furthermore, though, because a whole support system has been built to prop up the deception, the principality (strongman) must first be deposed and the structure he rules (stronghold) must be dissolved before truth can reign in liberty.

A person or nation deceived for any of these four reasons does not recognize the deception and will proliferate the lie as if it were the truth. This is how the devil's communication network functions. The believers of the falsehood unwittingly become transmitters of demonic deception.

SATAN'S TRANSMISSION TOWERS

There is a far more sinister means of demonic transmission than those described above. Within any demonically inspired religion or ideology are key individuals that become communication mediums. These cultic figures knowingly or unknowingly hear directly from demons, speaking and acting in accord with a satanic script. These "transmission towers" and their rituals help convey and augment the devil's deceptions. Much demonic activity is centered on them, and their rise to power seems proportionate to their ability to deceive. The weapon they seem to fear most is the truth; they will go to extraordinary lengths to corrupt the truth and to prevent the truth from being told.

As intercessors, we must interrupt the flow of demonic communication by praying tactical prayers for the souls of men and by praying strategic prayers not against flesh and blood but "against principalities, against powers, against the rulers of the darkness of this age, against spiritual hosts of wickedness in the heavenly places" (Ephesians 6:12 NKJV). Therefore, take up the whole armor of God and pray!

)(APPLICATION)(

KEY POINTS

(1) Strategic conclusions are based on the flow and availability of information.
(2) Warfare's direction, duration, and intensity are dictated by those who regulate information flow.
(3) The governing of information flow depends heavily on the worldview

filters through which people select and interpret information.

(4) The devil knows and broadcasts the lies people love most.

(5) Propaganda is effective because it broadcasts the lies people want to hear.

(6) A deceived person does not know he is deceived.

(7) There are at least four reasons people listen to lies:

  (a) Because they have been given no clear alternative

  (b) Because the lie is more convenient to believe than the truth

  (c) Because the devil has distorted the truth enough to make it false but not enough to make it disagreeable

  (d) Because the lie is so fantastically blatant that, in our naïveté, we cannot imagine that it could be false.

(8) Cultic individuals become the devil's transmission towers, and their rituals help convey and augment his deceptions.

SPIRITUAL RECONNAISSANCE

(1) What media does the devil seem to prefer for spreading his propaganda in our region? (Print, visual, audio, et al.)

(2) Through which leaders are these lies most often broadcast?

(3) Is there a group of people who seem more susceptible than others to these lies and methods?

PERSONALIZE IT

(1) What media does the devil seem to prefer for spreading his propaganda in my mind and heart?

(2) Through which individuals are these lies most often broadcast?

(3) Am I more susceptible to some lies and methods of deception than I am to others? What are they?

)(4)(

TARGETING DEMONIC CONVEYANCES

IN THIS WORLD, THE DEVIL'S POWER
AND INFLUENCE ARE CONVEYED
THROUGH PEOPLE.

VIRAL CARRIERS

In the natural realm, transportation occurs by land, by sea, or by air. In the spiritual realm, which is not limited to material space, demonic ideas and powers are conveyed by different but corresponding means. The devil is known as "the prince of the power of *the air*" (Ephesians 2:2 NKJV), and those he inspires traverse *land and sea* to make one proselyte more a son of hell than they themselves are (see Matthew 23:15).

Demons are not omnipresent—they can only be in one place at one time. But their influence, like a virus, can be carried in people's hearts and minds and can be transmitted to others. Though physically closed doors do not hinder demons, spiritually open doors definitely help them. When we leave the doors of our hearts open and unguarded to the world's influences, we can expect unwanted guests.

By carrying them around, we become carriers of their "spiritual viruses." When we close the doors of our hearts to everything not of God, we hinder and repulse the devil's advance not only in our own lives but also in the lives of those we influence. The stewardship of our spiritual doors requires daily vigilance and concrete accountability.

THE AIRWAVES

The devil assaults us and our families daily through radio, television, and other media. One researcher found that the average father spends only thirty-eight seconds a day of quality time with each of his children. Meanwhile, by the time his child is grown and ready to leave home, he or she will have witnessed over 38,000 murders on television and will have watched more than 11,000 hours of music videos (as much time as spent in school). And who can say what indoctrination has occurred through CDs, mp3s, radio, and the Internet?

Day in and day out, our children listen to lyrics they barely understand, performed by artists dedicated to the pursuit of worldly lusts and serving the prince and powers of the air. Who is discipling our children? Their dad or the devil? Their mom or the media?

Hinduism was almost unknown in the West until it was imported through the music and lives of the Beatles. The cult of Scientology, which employs mind-control techniques designed to gain control over money and souls, was virtually unknown until Tom Cruise, John Travolta, and Kirstie Alley made it a household term. How many other doctrines of devils are being similarly popularized?

TRANSIENT LEADERSHIP

Every media personality is a transient leader over whom we have no power. We don't know them personally. We don't know their past. We can't see their lifestyle or hold them accountable for what they say, do, or believe. Yet without verifying the accuracy of their perspective, many of us willingly allow them to influence us in the court of our personal opinion. They become authorities in our lives by virtue of being above our personal accountability.

That is the nature of a transient leader. He holds power by virtue of his ability to remain one step ahead of accountability. If accountability should catch up with him, he loses power. This ability is an occult power that can mask itself under a veneer of religion, behind a wall of wealth, or under cover of a culture. It remains remote by virtue of its inaccessibility.

While in Russia, I (Michael) once counseled a pastor who was having problems with his son. The son was so disobedient and inattentive to both mother and father that I was prompted to ask about the boy's daily regimen. The issue became obvious when I was told that he was daily watching between four and six hours of TV while interacting only six to ten minutes daily with Mom and Dad. I asked them, "Who is discipling your son, you or your television?" Parenthood is not an optional responsibility that we can delegate.

CULTURAL DISPLACEMENT

Indoctrination does not occur only through the airwaves. In Matthew 23:15, the sea is used to symbolize peoples and nations. In this age of mass movement and massive unrest, whole people groups being displaced to remote locations bring with them their demonic doctrines and their "household gods." Through sheer numbers, their beliefs become pervasive in areas where before they had been rare. Hence, in Germany and in England, there is a growing Islamic population introducing the Qur'an to nations that had formerly been leaders of Christian reformation. Their success is not so much due to the merits of Islam as to the failure of Christians to express the merits of God's Word—more on the passivity of the Christian church than on the activity of the Islamic world.

Twenty years ago I (Eddie) would have considered this unthinkable: Today, within three blocks of our U.S. Prayer Center office is a Hindu community, complete with temple. Within three miles are two Muslim mosques, one Sunni and one Shi'a. Immigrants have imported more than their families and possessions. They've imported their heathen worship and are enlarging demonic networks under our very noses.

When we failed to take the gospel of Christ to the nations, God sent the nations to us. We are faced with a confrontation not unlike Elijah facing the prophets of Baal. The question today is: "Which god will answer with fire from heaven?"

When the Sunni mosque in our neighborhood was being built, each weekday after taking my youngest daughter to school I would drive by and prayer-walk their property. After their building was "dried in," the contractor would see me drive up and would throw me the key. He assumed I was part of "the church"; he actually thought he was building a church! I would then enter the mosque and pray through each room and the tower.

As it reached completion, I wrote a letter of apology for the medieval crusades in which millions of Muslims were slaughtered in the name of Christ. I had the apology written calligraphically on parchment, took it to the five closest evangelical churches, and asked the pastors to sign it with me. Then I placed it into a gold frame and presented it to the imam. He was moved to tears and asked me to speak at the mosque's grand opening. Since then, I've developed a meaningful relationship with one of its elders. He is very near a decision to trust Christ.

Instead of evangelizing those who've come to dwell among us, that they might be like Christ, we tend to affirm them as they are and eventually allow ourselves to be influenced by their beliefs. We become like them. It's easier and less confrontational to do so and to avoid mentioning "Christ, and Him crucified," but it's also eternally devastating. While we joyfully anticipate eternity with God in heaven, those without the gospel are destined for a hellish eternity apart from Him. It's hard to take a stand for Christ in a contrary and violent world, but it's also the only right and merciful thing to do. God expects no less from His children.

DEFILED BY SIN

Finally, the devil's doctrines are spread over land. God, speaking to Moses at the burning bush, told him to remove his shoes, for he was standing on holy ground. But throughout the Old Testament there are references to "defiled land," unholy ground. We are told that land is defiled, for instance, by broken covenants, idol worship, adultery, and the shedding of innocent blood. God says in Ezekiel 22:30, "I looked for a man among them who would build up the wall and stand before me in the gap *on behalf of the land* so I would not have to destroy it, but I found none" (NIV).

A nation is defiled by the sins of its inhabitants. Sin perpetuates demonic depravity.

> The earth is also polluted by its inhabitants, for they transgressed laws, violated statutes, broke the everlasting covenant. Therefore, a curse devours the earth, and those who live in it are held guilty. (Isaiah 24:5–6)

The sins of our nations, clearly evident, are reflected everywhere in our land by our abuse of nature, by our waste of natural resources, and by the actions and lifestyles of our people. According to Hosea 4:1–3, the land itself mourns because of man's cursing, deception, murder, stealing, adultery, and violence so that bloodshed follows bloodshed. The blood of the innocent truly cries out to God from the ground.

Is there any hope? Yes!

If I shut up the heavens so that there is no rain, or if I command the locust to devour the land, or if I send pestilence among My people, and My people who are called by My name humble themselves and pray, and seek My face and turn from their wicked ways, then I will hear from heaven, will forgive their sin, and will heal their land. (2 Chronicles 7:13–14)

Intercessors, we must stand in the gap and "repent the land (turn from and sincerely apologize to God for the sins that have defiled the land, whether our own or others')."

Any successful military action requires the regulation of vehicular conveyances. The conveyances of the enemy must be hindered while those of the allies must be protected, multiplied, fueled, and improved. As intercessors we must take a careful look at our enemy's methods of conveyance, and we must regulate that activity through prayer and prophetic action.

APPLICATION

KEY POINTS

(1) Demons are not omnipresent. They can only be in one place at one time.

(2) Demonic influence, like a virus, is carried from one territory to another in people's hearts and minds.

(3) Spiritually open doors always invite unwanted guests.

(4) Hosts of unwanted guests become the carriers of their spiritual viruses.

(5) Spiritual stewardship requires daily vigilance and concrete accountability.

(6) Transient leaders hold power by avoiding accountability.

(7) The transient leader's ability to avoid accountability is an occult power.

(8) Mass media, left in the devil's hands, becomes a tool for the demonic counterfeit of omnipresence.

(9) Cultural displacement can become a tool for demonic migration.

(10) Sin legalizes demonic occupation.

SPIRITUAL RECONNAISSANCE

(1) Which transient leaders are exercising influence in our community?

(2) What doors into the community remain open to demonic influence?

(3) What are the TV-watching habits of the general populace?

(4) What people group has been displaced into my region, and what influence has their culture had on local culture?

(5) What regional sins are dominant and noteworthy, and how and where are they evident?

PERSONALIZE IT

(1) What transient leaders are exercising influence in my life?

(2) What doors into my life remain open to demonic influence?

(3) What are my TV-watching habits, and how do they compare to that of the general populace?

(4) What people group has been displaced into my region, and what influence has their culture had on me and on my family?

(5) What sins are dominant and noteworthy in my life, and how are they evident?

PRAYING FOR LEADERSHIP

THE DEVIL KNOWS THAT WHOEVER CONTROLS
THE PERSON OCCUPYING A POSITION OF
AUTHORITY CONTROLS THE PEOPLE UNDER
HIM. THEREFORE, THE DEVIL'S EFFORTS ARE
INTENSELY FOCUSED ON CORRUPTING PEOPLE
WHO OCCUPY LEADERSHIP POSITIONS.

Therefore I exhort first of all that supplications, prayers, intercessions, and giving of thanks be made for all men, for kings and all who are in authority, that we may lead a quiet and peaceable life in all godliness and reverence. (1 Timothy 2:1–2 NKJV)

POSITIONS OF AUTHORITY

All authority belongs to God and is delegated by Him to accomplish His will. However, authority is placed on positions of leadership and not on men. When we pray for those in authority, we pray for those who occupy positions of leadership in our community.

The devil knows that whoever controls the person occupying the position of authority controls the people he leads. So the devil is intently focused on corrupting those in positions of leadership.

Our responsibility to pray for our leaders is twofold:

▸ We must certainly pray for our *church leaders*.

▸ We must also pray for our *community leaders*.

If we fail to pray for church leaders, they and their ministries will have little or no effect on our communities. If we fail to pray for community leaders, they will persecute the church through whom God's blessings are intended to flow into a community. We dare not neglect to pray for *all who are in authority*. But how should we pray for our leaders?

IDENTIFY THE LEADERS

First, we must identify the leaders in our communities and churches. Unfortunately, many Christians are unaware of the names and policies of their elected officials. If we don't know who they are, how can we pray effectively for them?

But we must do more than know about them; whenever possible, we must also get to know them personally. It is much easier to pray for a person than for a picture. Our research can draw a mental picture, yet we won't pray for them as effectively as we should until we know them.

Of course, this begs the question: "How can I know (for example) the president or a member of Congress personally?" Not everyone can. But when we cannot know the leader personally, we should pray for those that do. I (Eddie) live in Houston, home of former president George Bush and his wife, Barbara. They're the parents of our president George W. Bush, and although I've never met the president or his parents, several of my friends have. Some of them know him very well. I can pray for them and for their influence in his life.

UNDERSTAND POSITIONAL PRESSURES

Second, we must understand the specific pressures of their leadership. Who is trying to exert ungodly influence to achieve ulterior and ungodly motives through them? How do the business, political, and religious communities relate to them? What expectations are placed upon them by these groups, and what is the extent of their authority to respond to these expectations? Is continuation in their position jeopardized by nonconformity to these desires? Is anyone praying for them on a regular basis?

PERSONAL DYNAMICS

Third, we must understand the dynamics of their personal lives. What are their ambitions, desires, and disappointments? What strains are placed on their lives as a result of their leadership responsibilities? How do events in their personal lives affect their decisions as leaders? How can we pray to minimize these stressful dynamics?

GENERALSHIP AND THE CHAIN OF COMMAND

Webster's defines *strategy* as "generalship; the science or art of combining and employing the means of war in planning and directing large military movements and operations" (*Webster's Encyclopedic Unabridged Dictionary of the English Language*). *Generalship* implies skill as commander of a large military force or unit. Command implies obedience, obedience implies relationship, and relationships imply people. If there are no people, there is no relationship, and if there are no relationships, the general commands no one. Strategy is built on a chain of command that requires covenant relationships within a nation's military forces.

One of Satan's key tactics is to disrupt the chain of command. Because relationships are strategic gates of influence that affect many people, they must be guarded at all costs. Chain of command is nothing more than strategic influence built on covenant relationships. Your relationships reflect your strategic influence. Thus, relationships are the key ingredient in any effective strategy, and Satan tries diligently to corrupt them, especially relationships among leaders.

It can be said without fear of contradiction that the higher the leader, the more effort Satan will use to corrupt his strategic relationships. Accordingly, one of the most effective strategies we can employ against the devil is praying for our leaders. It wears the devil out. And as you can imagine, a lot of his effort likewise goes into preventing the saints from praying for their leaders.

This is far more than a religious obligation; it is a strategic assault on Satan's plan, which is to ruin lives through corrupt leadership. If we pretend that such demonic designs for our leaders do not exist, one day we'll wake up and find that we ourselves have become slaves to the depravity we hate. We will awaken to the thunder of tyranny and be forced to march to the drumbeat of lies, prejudice, wickedness, and sin. We MUST pray for our leaders!

APPLICATION

KEY POINTS

(1) Christians have a twofold responsibility to pray for both those in positions of church leadership and those in positions of community leadership.

   (a) First, identify and personally get to know the leaders in your community and churches.

(b) Second, familiarize yourself with their positional pressures.

(c) Third, understand the dynamics of their personal lives.

(2) Relationships are strategic gates of influence affecting masses of people and must be guarded at all costs.

(3) Chain of command is nothing more than strategic influence built on covenant relationships.

(4) The higher the leader, the more effort Satan will employ to corrupt his strategic influence.

(5) Much demonic effort is invested in preventing the saints from praying for their leaders.

SPIRITUAL RECONNAISSANCE

(1) What positions of influence in our community might the devil want most to corrupt or occupy?

(2) Who are the religious leaders occupying positions of influence in our community?

(3) Who are the political leaders occupying positions of influence in our community?

(4) What are the most obvious positional pressures that leaders in our community might face, and what or who is the source of those pressures?

(5) What are the most obvious personal pressures facing leaders in our community?

PERSONALIZE IT

(1) What positions of influence in my personal life might the devil most want to corrupt?

(2) What religious pressures do I face, and from whom?

(3) What political pressures do I face, and from whom or from what source?

(4) What are the most obvious positional pressures I face on the job or at home, and who or what is the source of those pressures?

(5) What are the most obvious personal pressures I face?

TARGETING SUPPLY

NO ONE EVER HAS

ENOUGH TIME OR ENOUGH MONEY.

I n the spring of 1988, I (Michael) was about to realize a dream
for which I'd prayed for more than a year. I was being sent as a
missionary to Venezuela. I only had two problems: not enough
money and not enough time to get the money needed. It was Saturday morning, the day my congregational leaders would announce
that in one week I was being sent out as their first missionary. How
were they to know I was completely broke?

As I prayed, I began to complain to God. "Don't you understand? They're going to announce publicly that I am leaving as a
missionary for Venezuela! I don't have any money. I don't even have
a ticket. God, how can you do this to me? How can you put me
through such humiliation? I thought you loved me."

At that moment a still, small voice asked, *Is there anything that
you can be thankful for?* One little question is all it took for the Holy
Spirit to convict me of my sin and turn around my thinking. I
repented and began to remember all the Lord had done to prepare
me for that day. As I praised and thanked Him for everything I

could think of, a great joy and deep peace settled in my heart. I did have something for which to be thankful. I had something far more valuable than time or money. I had faith! From that day I would begin to learn one of the hallmark lessons of my life: You don't get a miracle until you need one. That morning I got my miracle.

When I arrived at our Messianic Jewish congregation, I was greeted by my travel agent and handed a ticket. "You can pay me for it after the service," she said. I was glad I had until then—I still had no money.

Finally, the time for my ordination came; I was prayed over and officially sent out. As I was leaving the platform and wondering what I'd soon have to say to my travel agent, the pastor called me back up. He had an envelope in his hand. Truthfully, I do not remember what he said, but I remember trying to keep my eyes off that envelope. I remember taking it and returning to my seat, where I peeked inside. To my great relief I discovered a check that would cover the cost of my ticket and give me eleven dollars besides. I could have shouted!

After the service I endorsed the check and handed it to my agent. I walked out with eleven dollars to my name, a ticket in my Bible, and a smile as wide as Texas across my face. All the following week I received money from unexpected sources, and by the time I left for Venezuela, I had over $1,800. Money is not a problem for God, and God is always on time!

TIME AND MONEY

In the natural world, there are two sought-after supplies no one ever seems to have enough of: *time* and *money*. The devil wants to control them both and will go to extraordinary lengths to keep them out of the hands of believers.

Meanwhile, he makes time and money very accessible to those

who would do his bidding. If it were not for the grace of God, believers would face a life of poverty and a mean and meaningless existence enslaved by time. But by God's grace the riches of heaven are at the disposal of those who have faith to apprehend them, and time is only a hiccup in our eternity with Him.

THE VALUE OF TIME

Of these two essential supplies, time is far more valuable. All the money in the world is worthless if we don't have time to use it. When considering our strategic and tactical prayer targets in that regard, we must give this principle preeminence. *Time is worth more than money!*

The devil knows this and will formulate time-robbing strategies to prevent us from maximizing our time for God. He will even give us more money if he thinks it will distract us from using our time wisely. He is watching to see how much time we spend spending money instead of preaching the gospel. We Christians must be careful that our concern for the things of this world does not choke off our fruitfulness for the kingdom of God.

RETURN ON INVESTMENT

Money is a renewable resource. Time is not. Though fortunes have been won and lost many times in the course of history, commerce continues unabated. With enough money you can buy anything except more time. But money is only useful if we use it. And the best use of money, the use that will bring the greatest return for our investment, is to extend God's kingdom. Jesus said, "Make friends for yourselves by means of the wealth (mammon) of unrighteousness, so that when it fails, they will receive you into the eternal dwellings" (Luke 16:9). Who besides the saved live in eternity and can welcome you into eternal dwellings?

FAITH: THE MISSING FACTOR?

It's been said that unbelievers buy and sell while believers give and receive. Such generosity requires faith. Faith is the essential ingredient in God's economy. It is by faith that Christians tithe, give to the poor, and make investment decisions. It is by faith that we give to missions. Our spiritual supply of faith supersedes our natural-world limitations. We believe, and God, according to our faith, supplies our needs.

When choosing strategic and tactical prayer targets in the realm of supply and demand, we must consider three things:

(1) Time is limited and more valuable than money.
(2) Money is only useful if we use it, and it's best used to preach the gospel.
(3) God grants to us a faith supply that supersedes our natural limitations.

So, when we pray, let us . . .

▸ Pray against the devil's tactics that rob us and others of our time.

▸ Ask God to supply the financial resources necessary to expand His kingdom through our lives.

▸ Pray that Christians would properly evaluate their use of money and would begin to give, by faith, toward that which brings the greatest return.

OUR ROOT PRIORITIES

We must understand: Our checkbook reflects our priorities. Less than one-tenth of one percent of total Christian income is given to foreign missions each year; that's less than one of every thousand dollars. Tragically, this is less than the amount lost each year to ecclesiastical crime (theft of church property or offerings by members or leaders). The devil is far cleverer in his use of money than are many believers.

Meanwhile, regarding our use of time, the average Great Commission Christian (who believes in actively working toward the Commission's completion) spends less than 2 percent of their life sharing their faith.

Several years ago, I (Eddie) attended a national conference on world evangelism in a midwestern city. On my way to the final plenary session, I stopped at the gift shop to purchase some mints.

There I met Rasheed, from Pakistan. I asked him, "Has anyone this week shared with you the good news of Jesus Christ and His salvation?" Rasheed shook his head. I took the time to present Christ and His gospel, and Rasheed prayed to receive Christ!

When I arrived at the meeting, a long discussion developed on strategies the American church might employ to complete the Great Commission. Finally I said politely, yet firmly, "Gentlemen, the longer we sit in rooms like this, discussing the problem, while ignoring people like Rasheed—the young Pakistani man who manages the gift shop across the hall, who just gave his heart to Christ—the further we will be from the goal."

It's clear that if we want to see strategic gains in our use of time and money for the kingdom, we must first prayerfully reverse this trend. *If, as we say, "our priority is saving lost souls," our gifts of time and money should more meaningfully reflect it.*

APPLICATION

KEY POINTS

(1) You don't get a miracle until you need one.
(2) Money is not a problem for God, and God is always on time!
(3) The devil goes to great lengths to keep time and money out of the

hands of believers, but he makes these accessible to those who would do his bidding.

(4) Time is limited and more valuable than money.

(5) Demonic time-robbing strategies prevent you from maximizing your time for God.

(6) Money is a renewable resource. Time is not.

(7) Money is only useful if we use it, and it's best used to preach the gospel.

(8) Heaven's riches are at the disposal of those who have faith to apprehend them.

(9) Faith is an essential ingredient in God's economy.

(10) Faith is a supernatural supply that supersedes our natural limitations.

(11) Our use of time and money should reflect our root priorities.

SPIRITUAL RECONNAISSANCE

(1) What are my community's top three priorities for its use of time and money?

(2) What are my Christian community's top three priorities for its use of time and money?

(3) How well does the secular and Christian communities' use of time and money reflect their stated priorities?

(4) In what specific ways do the secular and Christian communities' use of time and money reflect their abundance of faith or lack of faith?

PERSONALIZE IT

(1) What are my top three priorities for use of time and money?

(2) What three Christian ministries receive most of my time and money?

(3) How well does my use of time and money reflect my stated priorities?

(4) To what degree does my use of time and money reflect my abundance of faith or lack of faith?

TARGETING STRATEGIC POSITIONS

WHEN ENGAGED IN BATTLE, EVERY ARMY FIGHTS TO POSSESS THE HIGH PLACES.

Hig h places" provide one or more of the following strategic characteristics:

(1) A commanding view of the surrounding area
(2) An increased tactical assault capability
(3) The ability to control safe passage from one area to another
(4) Inaccessibility to enemy assault.

When engaged in battle, every army fights to possess the high places. Destroying a high place eliminates its strategic significance. Conquering a high place yields control of its strategic significance. From that position we can more effectively implement our own strategy and/or hinder the implementation of the enemy's. It's extremely important to occupy such strategic staging areas.

THE OUTER GATES

Strategic positions, high places, can also be called "the gates of the city." The basic types are (1) geographic, (2) political, (3) commercial, and (4) religious.

We call these four strategic positions "the outer gates." In addition to these, there are also four lesser strategic positions that we call "the inner gates." We'll look at those below; for now, know that the use of "inner gates" is dictated by and strengthens those occupying political, commercial, and religious positions in a (geographic) community.

GEOGRAPHIC GATES

Geographic gates are actual physical locations. Their convenience for the general public makes them profitable; commercial enterprises often seek to occupy them because they recognize their strategic importance. It's said that in the world of retail marketing there are three essential criteria: location, location, location! Sometimes a good place is more important than a good product, for without it you must have adequate incentive to draw people to a bad location. In the same way, the locations of our ministries are of strategic importance; when we pray, we should ask God for the opportunity to occupy strategic geographic locations.

POLITICAL GATES

Political gates are "gates" of influence—positions of influence in a society. Because their occupiers make decisions and set legal and cultural precedents that establish the societal course, these positions are very strategic; people need influential favor and blessing for their endeavors. Intrinsically, the positions may not be profitable, but they create profitability through association with other people of influence. We ought to pray that such positions would be occupied by the righteous.

COMMERCIAL GATES

Commercial gates are gates of financial influence within a community. Those who occupy these places understand that all commerce depends on the exchange of money. It's assumed that any service or product can be bought for the right price, and a wealthy man has many friends whose influence he can purchase. The right to occupy geographic, political, or even religious positions can sometimes be obtained by financial influence. We'd do well to remember that the most profitable investment of money, the extension of God's kingdom, reaps eternal rewards. God will hold us accountable for the ethical use of the "talents" He's given us, and we should pray accordingly.

RELIGIOUS GATES

Religious gates are institutions that primarily exist to shape a people's worldview. Some exist not merely to transfer reliable spiritual information and increase knowledge but also to bend the use of information and knowledge toward achieving a specific religious or political end. Because people who occupy religious positions influence society's general worldview, these "places" can be extremely financially and politically profitable. The promoted paradigm beneficially or adversely affects both politics and commerce. Therefore, we must not neglect to pray for the righteousness of religious leaders.

THE INNER GATES

The four "inner gates" through which all society passes are (1) health and human services, (2) education, (3) mass media, and (4) culture. Those who occupy the inner and outer gates control the community's destiny. Thus we must pray that these gates would be controlled by righteous men and women who will act in accord with the will of God.

Because every member of society passes through these gates, they can be used to regulate and strengthen political, financial, and religious positions. Whereas you cannot enter a city except through the outer gates, you cannot wield lasting and widespread influence without standing in the inner gates.

The City Gates are places and/or systems of influence that regulate the flow and quality of people. Some are forbidden entry, while others are royally welcomed. Though some gates may be more familiar or common than others, every *citizen* will at some point pass through every gate.

Strategic Positions are gates and high places from which a people's destiny can be regulated. If the wicked occupy these positions, they will influence the people for harm; if the righteous occupy these positions, they will influence the people for good and will open the city's gates to God's blessings. Let us pray that those who occupy strategic positions would be righteous and that the wicked would not rule the hearts of men.

> *Lift up your heads, O gates,*
> *And be lifted up, O ancient doors,*
> *That the King of glory may come in!*
> *Who is the King of Glory?*
> *The Lord strong and mighty,*
> *The Lord mighty in battle.*
> *Lift up your heads, O gates,*
> *And lift them up, O ancient doors,*
> *That the King of Glory may come in!*
> *Who is this King of glory?*
> *The Lord of hosts,*
> *He is the King of glory. Selah.* (Psalm 24:7–10)

KEY POINTS

(1) High places possess one or more of these strategic characteristics:
    (a) A commanding view of the surrounding area
    (b) An increased tactical assault capability
    (c) The ability to control safe passage from one area to another
    (d) Inaccessibility to enemy assault

(2) Destroying a high place eliminates its strategic significance.

(3) Conquering a high place yields control of its strategic significance.

(4) The four basic types of "outer gate" strategic positions are:
    (a) geographic
    (b) political
    (c) commercial
    (d) religious

(5) The four basic "inner gate" strategic positions are:
    (a) health and human services
    (b) education
    (c) mass media
    (d) culture

(6) Those who occupy a community's inner and outer gates control its destiny.

(7) Whereas you cannot enter a city except through the outer gates, you cannot wield lasting and widespread influence without standing in the inner gates.

SPIRITUAL RECONNAISSANCE

(1) Where is our community's prime commercial and residential real estate?

(2) Who occupies our community's key political offices, and are any of these soon to be up for reelection?

(3) Who are our community's renowned businesspeople, and in what goods and services do they deal?

(4) Who are our community's key religious leaders, and what relationship do they have with key commercial and political leaders?

(5) Who is our community's chair of the board of education, and what positions on that board may be filled by members of the general public?

(6) What are our community's most prevalent cultures? Where do they meet, and who are their leaders?

(7) Who publishes the local newspaper, periodicals, and books, and who owns and operates the local radio and TV stations?

(8) Who are our community's health and human services providers?

PERSONALIZE IT

(1) Do I or a family member own prime commercial and residential real estate in my community that may be useful for God's purposes?

(2) Would I ever consider running for political office? If so, which office?

(3) Do I personally know any renowned businesspeople in my community? If not, how could I get to know them?

(4) Do I personally know any renowned religious leaders in my community? If not, how could I get to know them?

(5) Would I be willing to serve on the education board if the opportunity presented itself?

(6) How do my community's most prevalent cultures personally affect me, and would I be willing to become more involved with them?

(7) Am I aware of what's locally published and broadcasted?

(8) Do I personally know my community's health and human service providers? If not, how could I get to know them?

PART **2** S P I R I T U A L
S T R A T E G Y

UNIFIED COMMAND

IF YOU WISH TO REACH YOUR OBJECTIVE,
BOTH EYES MUST BE LOOKING IN
THE SAME DIRECTION.

T here was nothing particularly different about the afternoon
prayer meeting I (Michael) conducted at our mountain home
in El Valle, Venezuela. It included a few ministry friends and a pastor and his wife from El Vijia they'd wanted us to meet. However,
as we began to pray, our agreement in the Spirit gave us the sense
that this gathering was significant regarding our future ministry
there, and this eventually proved to be precisely the case. A few
weeks later, when we visited El Vijia, we were able to bring together
in one room thirty-two of the city's thirty-six pastors in a historic
meeting with lasting positive effects.

Now, weeks before, during the initial meeting, we were together
in God's presence. This was the launch of our plan to visit El Vijia
and bring a word regarding Israel to its pastors. Rarely had I experienced such unity while praying with those I'd recently met. While
the prayer time was memorable, more unforgettable was our final

"Amen!" As we said it, in unison, an earthquake shook the mountain, as if God were pronouncing it with us.

AGREE TOGETHER

Jesus mentions two ingredients that empower our prayer: agreement and togetherness.

> Again, I tell you that if two of you on earth *agree about anything* you ask for, it will be done for you by my Father in heaven. For where two or three *come together in my name*, there am I with them. (Matthew 18:19–20 NIV)

Notice we aren't commanded to agree about *everything*—that's never going to happen. Clearly, diversity is as much God's gift as unity. Besides, without diversity, unity wouldn't be necessary. When unity turns into uniformity, people can be robbed of individuality.

Several years ago I (Eddie) called a Baptist pastor to invite him to a city pastors' prayer meeting. When he agreed to come I added, "Why don't you bring Pastor John (a pastor whose church was across the street) with you?"

"What? Pastor John? He's an Assembly of God pastor! This isn't a *Baptist* prayer meeting?"

"No," I explained. "It's a *pastors'* prayer meeting."

"I can't pray with someone with whom I disagree."

I replied, "Alice and I disagree about a lot of things, but we can still pray together!"

(Believe me, his attitude isn't the attitude of most Baptist pastors, nor is it specific to them. I've found variations of it in other denominations and nondenominational groups.)

Unity isn't uniformity. Followers of Christ, regardless of denominational affiliation, usually agree that Jesus Christ, who is God, came to earth as a man, was born of a virgin, lived a sinless life, died an atoning death, was raised from the dead, ascended into heaven, and is coming again. This agreement is the basis on which we come together to do kingdom business.

This is the essence of the apostles' doctrine, the beliefs for which they willingly laid down their lives. Perhaps we should distinguish between doctrines based on our opinions and interpretations (which are fine), and our doctrines based on the person of Christ, for which we should be willing to die. It is here that our unity is anchored.

Let's look once more at the words of Jesus:

> Again, I tell you that if two of you on earth *agree about anything* you ask for, it will be done for you by my Father in heaven. For where two or three *come together in my name*, there am I with them. (Matthew 18:19–20 NIV)

Suppose you were given the world's most expensive sports car. "Great!" you say.

One problem: all four wheels are pointed and locked in different directions. Your dream car is about as useful as a fancy garden planter—it's going nowhere. Unity means all four wheels pointing in the same direction; this congruency is critical to arriving at our intended destination.

The people in Genesis 11:6 are building the Tower of Babel when God comes down to check it out, and He says in effect, "They are *one people*, and all of them *speak the same language*. That is why they can do this. Now they will *be able to do anything they plan to.*"

Here we learn an important biblical principle: *Unity enables.*

Thousands of years later Jesus says, "Every kingdom that fights against itself will be destroyed. Every city or family that is divided against itself will not stand" (Matthew 12:25 NIrV). That's the other side of the coin: *Disunity disables.*

THE MINISTRY OF RECONCILIATION

Paul writes,

> All things are of God, who hath reconciled us to himself by Jesus Christ, and *hath given to us the ministry of reconciliation;* to wit, that God was in Christ, reconciling the world unto himself. . . . We are ambassadors for Christ, as though God did beseech you by us: we pray you in Christ's stead, be ye reconciled to God. (2 Corinthians 5:18–20 KJV)

God reconciled us to himself so we could reconcile others to Him. King David prayed,

> Create in me a clean heart. . . .
> Then will I teach transgressors thy ways;
> and sinners shall be converted unto thee.
> (Psalm 51:10, 13 KJV)

God forgives us of our sins so He can forgive the sins of others. His forgiveness qualifies us for the evangelization of sinners. Because our hearts are clean, we teach transgressors His ways, and they are converted.

Along the same line, this powerful and revealing prayer of Jesus was prayed for His disciples, which includes us:

> Father, I pray that all of them will be one, just as you are in me and I am in you. I want them also to be in us. *Then the world will believe* that you have sent me. I have given them the glory you gave me. I did this *so they would be one, just as we are one.* I will be in them, just as you are in me. *I want them to be brought together perfectly as one. This will let the world know that you sent me. It will also show the world that you have loved those you gave me,* just as you have loved me. (John 17:21–23 NIrV)

Four significant points:

(1) The world will never believe the gospel we preach until we preach it in unity. (v. 21)

(2) Jesus came to earth to make us one, as He and the Father are one. (v. 22)

(3) His plan is that we be brought together *perfectly* as one. Not in heaven, but right here. (see v. 24)

Why?

(4) The world will know by *our unity* that God so loved *them* that He gave His only begotten Son. (3:16)

God has given us the ministry of reconciliation. For centuries we've preached to the world, "Be reconciled to God," and they've looked at the divisions among us and rightly said, "Who are you to preach to us? Why should we be reconciled to God when you're not reconciled with each other?" *A disabled church will never win a disabled world.*

SINGULAR FOCUS

If we wish to reach our objective, we must be looking in the same direction, focusing on the same thing. Unless our eyes are under the unified command of our brain, we cannot see clearly. From what our eyes observe, our brain defines the *singular objective* toward which our bodies move. Without the help of our brain, which performs many different functions, we will not be able to define our goals or determine our target. Unity among men is "group focus."

When you pick up a map to plan a trip, what's the first thing you look for? Current location. You must first know where you are, then you look for your destination and prepare to make the trip. Now you've established your goal.

An undefined goal is an unachievable goal. If you don't know where you're going, you'll neither know which road to take nor when you've arrived. So it is with prayer. Without a clear objective, our prayers will accomplish nothing.

Just as the brain assesses what the eyes see and thus determines the target, pastoral leadership must define the prayer goals (targets) for a church. Regardless of whether our targets are strategic or tactical, it's imperative that they are specific, and we must have a definite strategy for reaching them. With indefinite goals, people's minds will wander, they will eventually lose interest, and the prayer ministry will dissipate. With an ill-defined strategy, people will unconsciously sense they are wasting time and effort on an indefinite or unachievable goal.

One night I (Eddie) was in a college prayer meeting. The gymnasium was filled with passionate intercessors praying for revival and spiritual awakening in our city. Then a young student stood to pray. "Lord," he said tearfully, "I will neither eat nor sleep until every man, woman, boy, and girl in Houston, Texas, has come to a saving knowledge of Jesus Christ!"

I knew his heart. Although I'm a granddaddy today, I too was once a college freshman. I slipped to his side following the meeting and said, "Billy, I appreciate your passionate prayer for souls tonight; but I think it's only fair to tell you that the prayer you prayed cannot be answered."

"Why?" he asked, "Why would you say that?"

"It cannot be answered, because Christ himself has told us that the road to heaven is narrow, and few will find it."

This kind of spiritual arm-twisting prayer is unfair to God. If He answers, He sets a precedent for a mediator other than Jesus Christ. If He doesn't answer, this young man's eventual death (from not eating or sleeping) casts a shadow both against the nature of Christianity and against the character of God.

When we pray, we must first define a specific, achievable objective—a reasonable goal.

REALISTIC GOALS AND VERIFIABLE RESULTS

Never forget, our main goal is not merely to identify prayer targets but to reach them. Good leaders set *realistic goals* when they select targets. Nothing is more frustrating for a battle-weary prayer warrior than interceding for hours, months, days, and years and never realizing results. Results in the life of an intercessor are often the only reward he or she ever receives. To obtain verifiable results, leaders must select definite and achievable goals.

Unverifiable results are not results, they are coincidences. Praying for a healthy man to get healed is a waste of time—after prayer, we can't claim his healing unless he was verifiably sick. No true intercessor is comforted by such "miracles." Intercessors want *verifiable results*, and so does God. Hence, the goals leaders set must be achievable. It's impossible to verify progress toward an unachievable goal.

Perhaps one of the most overlooked aspects of strategic prayer is our failure to verify results. It seems to me (Eddie) that we typically pray our way from one problem to the next rather than from one solution to the next.

It is reported that when George Mueller died, his prayer journal yielded more than 50,000 answers to prayer. If we died, our journals might list 50,000 requests, because we tend to focus on *our requests*. Mueller focused on God's responses!

Consider for a moment. If you were God, whose prayer would you answer: the one who continually focused on his need, or the one who continually focused on your response? God loves praise. He does what He does for praise. Track, record, and celebrate His responses so you don't gradually move into dry, routine prayers rather than powerful divine experiences.

INCREMENTAL EXECUTION AND UNIFIED COMMAND

Know how to eat an elephant? One bite at a time! In some cases God directs us to pray for goals that can only be achieved incrementally. We often regard such prayers as prophetic because we can't fully comprehend how to reach our objective from where we presently stand. Such a massive mountain seems too big and too remote to be removed by our meager prayers. In these instances we must satisfy ourselves with achieving our goal in stages, step by step.

If our prayer objective seems fantastic, perhaps we should subdivide it into smaller, more measurable, more achievable goals. For instance, we can reach our city for Christ one block, one home, and one person at a time. In the same way, achieving a "prophetic prayer goal" sometimes requires *incremental execution* of smaller prayer goals. In this way we work toward our singular overriding prophetic objective one step at a time, and we pray in an orderly, unified, and strategic fashion.

It makes no sense for us to take step five before we've taken step one. Orderliness in prayer requires a *unified command*. Effective strategy requires unified command. That doesn't mean all prayer must proceed under one leader, but it does mean all praying leaders must be in unity. Leaders must agree on the essential objectives and on the order of priority.

As we press toward our prayer goal, our intermediate targets must also be identified and prioritized. Accomplishing this mammoth task of spiritual reconnaissance requires our reliance on the wisdom that comes from a multitude of counselors. We need to make war wisely; using the wisdom of joint reconnaissance reaches far beyond our singular observational ability.

Agreement in prayer is powerful. However, the true power of agreement isn't based upon one person's opinions or conclusions. Its strength is derived from the group's accumulated observations formulated into a singular, overriding, comprehensive, and achievable goal.

ESSENTIAL PRAYER STRATEGY

In summary, we could define our essential prayer strategy as "the incremental execution of a singular realistic (achievable) objective, under unified command, with verifiable results." Any strategy we formulate must take these elements into account; any strategy that neglects one or more will be weakened.

▶ a singular, overriding objective

▶ achievable goal

▶ unified command

▶ incremental execution

▶ verifiable result.

Accountability and integrity are refreshing in a day when Christians sometimes make preposterous, unverifiable ministry claims. The last church Alice and I served as pastors was built on *strategic prayer*. People from other churches in town, including pastors, visited our prayer meetings, largely because they were measurably productive. We didn't select targets and assignments, pray them through, then skip the results. We followed up our assaults by identifying, recording, and reporting the results. For example, we'd prayed for the closing of Houston's strip joints and exotic dance clubs and seen fifteen or twenty shut down within three months. We were privileged to lead one exotic dancer to Christ. She left the industry, returned to her family, and enrolled in college.

Imagine the excitement such a report brings to the hearts of committed warriors! People came from all over because they could see the *measurable effect* of our praying. When a measurable effect wasn't reported, we admitted we'd missed the target or misunderstood the assignment, and we looked for ways to improve.

APPLICATION

KEY POINTS

(1) Undefined goals are unachievable.
(2) Leadership must define the prayer goals of a church.
(3) Leaders who want verifiable results must select definite, realistic goals.
(4) God often directs us to pray for goals that can only be achieved incrementally.
(5) All effective strategy requires unified command.
(6) Unified command ensures orderliness in prayer.
(7) Prayer leaders must agree on essential objectives and on priority.
(8) Any strategy we formulate must take into account these essential elements:

> ▸ a singular, overriding objective
>
> ▸ achievable goal
>
> ▸ unified command
>
> ▸ incremental execution
>
> ▸ verifiable result.

SPIRITUAL RECONNAISSANCE

(1) What are the common objectives of Christian leaders throughout our community?
(2) Do these objectives contain agreed-upon definitions of goals and strategies?
(3) Are the defined goals realistic? If not, what would make them more achievable?

(4) How will the Christian community be able to verify that it has achieved the desired results?

(5) What are the first three steps toward the execution of each goal?

(6) Among the leaders, is there one apostolic figure whose opinion everyone respects?

PERSONALIZE IT

(1) What are my personal objectives toward Christian maturity, and with whom in my community are they common?

(2) Do these objectives contain definitions of goals and strategies that can be agreed upon by others?

(3) Are the defined goals realistic? If not, what would make them more achievable?

(4) How will I be able to verify that I've achieved the desired results?

(5) What are the first three steps toward the execution of each goal?

(6) Is there an apostolic figure in my life who can guide me toward reaching those goals?

)(9)(

STRATEGIC DIVERSION

DIVERSION IS MORE THAN A MOMENTARY
DISTRACTION; IT IS THE PURSUIT OF FALSE OR
LESSER GOALS THAT DRAW ESSENTIAL
RESOURCES AWAY FROM THE POINT OF
THEIR MOST STRATEGIC IMPACT.

I n a military sense, any activity that draws resources away from where they'll have the most impact is a diversion. This is the battle principle of *divide and conquer*. Strategic diversion is a cornerstone of an efficient campaign.

In the modern era, strategic diversion was a cornerstone of the Bolshevik Revolution's success. Knowing that Czar Nicholas II's internal military force was sufficient to quell any attempted coup, Lenin went about diverting that force to interests outside the country. He traveled west to encourage Germany to intensify their activities on the Russian border; the increased activity forced Nicholas to minimize his internal security forces in order to send more troops to the front. The resulting shift was precisely the reaction

Lenin wanted. With the military sufficiently diversified, Lenin was able to mobilize a discontented populace to revolt against the Czar's weakened forces. The resultant communist era is testimony to his successful strategy.

We see a clear application of this strategy in Joshua's attack on the city of Ai (Joshua 8:1–23). At first, because of Achan's sin, the Israelites were defeated. But after they repented and renounced Achan's sin, God promised to deliver Ai into their hands and instructed Joshua to set an ambush.

Israel was to divide its military into two forces. One force would draw the people of Ai away from the city. When Ai's troops were sufficiently diverted to chasing the Israelites, the second force would attack the city. Joshua executed this strategy exactly as the Lord instructed, and here are the results:

> The men in ambush rose quickly from their place, and when he had stretched out his hand, they ran and entered the city and captured it; and they quickly set the city on fire. When the men of Ai turned back and looked, behold, the smoke of the city ascended to the sky, and they had no place to flee this way or that, for the people who had been fleeing to the wilderness turned against the pursuers. When Joshua and all Israel saw that the men in ambush had captured the city and that the smoke of the city ascended, they turned back and slew the men of Ai. (vv. 19–21 NIV)

Joshua employed two strategies: *diversion* and *distraction*. He drew the people away from the city through diversion. They were defeated when they turned from the battle to see their burning city.

We shouldn't assume that this effective strategy went unnoticed by the surrounding nations. Note this: We shouldn't assume that our own innovative strategies against demonic forces will work the same every time we employ them. The enemy usually learns from his mistakes and will later use our own strategies against us. We must remain vigilant to the Holy Spirit's voice when establishing strategy. He alone knows which one is best applied at any given time.

DISTRACTION AND DIVERSION

Distraction causes a momentary lapse in attention that grants us the opportunity to take decisive action. Distraction doesn't weaken our enemy but provides an opening for us to catch him off guard.

Diversion is more than a momentary distraction. It's essentially the pursuit of a false or lesser goal. A diversion actually weakens our opponent so that regardless of whether or not he's distracted, he will be unable to respond with sufficient force to protect his interests.

In the spiritual realm, Satan commonly employs both diversion and distraction. The effectiveness of his efforts depends upon the level of our *vigilance*. It's important for intercessors to discern whether the obvious attack is focused on the true objective or is merely a distraction or a diversion from a more important front.

My (Michael's) experience has shown that Satan usually has an ulterior motive and a Plan B. So regardless of whether the obvious battle is focused on a main objective, we should always seek to discover his ulterior motives. Because of the danger that lack of vigilance poses, diversion and distraction are significant prayer targets.

KEY POINTS

(1) Simply stated, the principle of strategic diversion says, "Divide and conquer!"

(2) Distraction does not weaken an opposing force; it only causes a

momentary lapse of attention that grants opportunity for gaining an advantage.

(3) Diversion actually weakens an opposing force so that regardless of whether he's distracted, he will be unable to respond with sufficient force to guard his interests.

(4) Satan usually learns from his mistakes, and we should not assume that the effectiveness of our spiritual strategies will go unnoticed or that they'll work the same every time we employ them.

(5) We must remain vigilant to the Spirit's voice when establishing strategy.

(6) Intercessors must discern whether the obvious attack is focused on the true objective or merely a distraction or a diversion from a more important front.

(7) The threats that diversion and distraction pose are directly proportional to our lack of vigilance.

SPIRITUAL RECONNAISSANCE

(1) Are our local church's time, energy, and resources focused on a specific goal?

(2) What diversions seem to impede our local church from reaching this goal?

(3) What distractions are diverting our local church from focusing its attention on a specific goal?

(4) In what concrete areas do I feel my local church must be more vigilant?

PERSONALIZE IT

(1) Are my time, energy, and resources focused on a specific goal for the sake of my local church?

(2) What diversions seem to impede me from reaching this goal?

(3) What distractions are diverting me from focusing my attention on this specific goal?

(4) In what concrete areas do I feel I must be more vigilant?

THE PREEMPTIVE STRIKE

IT IS ONLY LOGICAL FOR AN ENEMY TO
ATTEMPT TO KNOCK US OFF BALANCE OR TO
MESS WITH OUR FOCUS JUST BEFORE WE MOVE
FORCEFULLY AGAINST HIM.

Consistently, throughout my ministry, I (Michael) have noticed that as I prepare a major advance for God's kingdom, Satan launches a preemptive strike. Though in the beginning I was often caught off guard, this tactic no longer surprises me. In fact, I'm surprised when he attempts nothing. It's only logical for him to attempt to knock us off balance or to mess with our focus just before we move forcefully against him. Because I now understand the logic behind the preemptive strike, I always try to sabotage his preemptive plans through *preventive prayer*. Preventive prayer requires a special sensitivity to the Holy Spirit.

The temptation of the natural mind is to dismiss as foolish something for which there is no tangible evidence. This is precisely the situation in the spiritual realm. There is no tangible evidence for something that hasn't yet happened—there is only a Spirit-led premonition and a nagging, unexplainable urgency to pray. When we do pray and nothing happens, we wonder whether or not we've heard clearly from the Spirit. When we don't pray and something does happen we wonder, "Why didn't I listen to the Spirit?"

If you don't know what I'm talking about, you're probably not an intercessor. Those involved in strategic-level spiritual warfare are familiar with this phenomenon; they've trained themselves to ignore the natural mind and to pray according to the Holy Spirit's leading.

Signs of a Preemptive Strike

Silence

Perhaps one of the most noticeable indicators of a preemptive strike is an unusual silence. There is calm before the storm so that the enemy can avoid arousing suspicion. Any unusual attention is unwanted.

There's always a battle going on in my mind whenever things seem to be going too well. On one hand I think, *Of course! I pray. I'm a child of God under His protection. I'm a man of faith. Of course things are going smoothly.* On the other I think, *Wait a minute, if I'm moving against the kingdom of darkness, why am I not experiencing any resistance?* Demonic silence can be ominous and unnerving. The absence of resistance is sometimes evidence that the enemy is secretly amassing a counterforce. In those circumstances, pay close attention to the Spirit's quiet voice that calls you to prayer. It could literally save your life and your ministry.

Distraction or Diversion

Another evidence is diversion or distraction. Commonly, in order to maximize the preemptive strike's effect, Satan will divert our attention and energy at the most strategic moment. This weakens our resistance and strains our vigilance. Then, while we're weak and inattentive, distraction opens the door for his strike. Don't jump to conclusions. *Train yourself to avoid spontaneous reaction to trouble or crisis.* Before you act, ask God for discernment and wait for His answer.

LEADERSHIP PURGE

A leadership purge always indicates impending change. That change may be for the better, or it may be for the worse. During a leadership purge, one should pay particular attention to what's going on in the spheres influenced by those positions and the people who occupy them.

Is the purge an attempt to consolidate power? Or is the leader genuinely interested in producing greater fruitfulness? Even when the purge is for the better, understand that the devil will attempt to disrupt the change and corrupt the transition so he can limit the benefits God intends. Situations like a leadership purge always merit vigilant prayer.

LEGAL ACTIVITY

Any unusual activity in the legal sphere of religious law is a warning sign of an impending strike against religious freedom. Often, legislators will change laws governing religious freedom in anticipation of having to justify the legality of a counter-religious action in the eyes of the public. This change is usually unpublicized or, if publicized, is usually given a benign title and only selectively explained. We must not allow our lack of vigilance to rob us of our liberty.

Especially in the West, because much of our lawmaking is based on Judeo-Christian beliefs, it's inconceivable to many that a law could be unjust. Where unjust and arbitrary laws are more commonplace, people may be less likely to assume that their elected officials will always have their best interests in mind. Some officials are talented, charismatic power brokers, social pawns whose own interests and ambitions preempt the interests of those who elected them. Unfortunately, clever and unrighteous people can and do pass clever and unjust laws for their own selfish ends.

Generally, when religious laws change, one should ask the question, "Why was this law changed?" Was there a legitimate and beneficent purpose for changing it? Will our freedoms be expanded or restricted? Who championed this change, and who opposed it? Why were they for or against it, and what spiritual issues most influenced them? When the legislature considers drafting a new law on religious freedom, if you hear one voice saying, "Pray!" and another saying, "Don't worry," it's always better to err on the side of prayer.

MEDIA ATTACKS

Legal attacks also are often geared to legitimize false accusations. This is especially apparent in the media. If an accusation appears there, whether or not it's true, someone will believe it. If the accusation is repeated often enough, the number of those who believe it will increase exponentially. A lie repeated often enough eventually becomes believable. So legal activity tied to the media should also be regarded as a possible warning of a preemptive strike.

KEY POINTS

(1) Sabotage your enemy's preemptive plans through *preventive prayer*.
(2) The temptation of the natural mind is to dismiss as foolish something for which there is not yet any tangible evidence.
(3) We must train ourselves to ignore the natural mind and to pray according to the Holy Spirit's leading.

(4) Signs of a preemptive strike:
  - (a) Silence: the absence of resistance is often evidence of the secret amassing of a counterforce.
  - (b) Distraction or Diversion: to maximize the preemptive strike's effect, Satan will divert our attention and energy at the most strategic moment.
  - (c) Leadership Purge: such a purge always indicates impending change.
  - (d) Legal Activity: unusual activity in the legal sphere of religious law is often a warning sign of an impending strike against religious freedom.
  - (e) Media Attacks: if a false "legal" accusation reaches the media, someone will believe it, and if it's repeated often enough, the number of those that believe it will increase.

SPIRITUAL RECONNAISSANCE

(1) What is the Holy Spirit saying to you and other Christian leaders and intercessors regarding the territory in which you live?
(2) Has there been an uneasy silence related to issues facing our community?
(3) Has there recently been a significant leadership change in the political, religious, commercial, or social gates of our city?
(4) Have there been recent and significant changes of law regarding the government of our community?
(5) What position, if any, has the media taken regarding important social issues our community is facing?

PERSONALIZE IT

(1) What is the Holy Spirit saying to me about my home or neighborhood?
(2) Has there been an uneasy silence concerning issues facing my home or neighborhood?
(3) Has a respected family member or neighbor recently moved into or out of my home or neighborhood?
(4) Have there been recent and significant zoning or policy changes in

my neighborhood or a covenant change in my home?

(5) What position have I taken regarding the home issues I personally face, and what position has my neighborhood taken regarding the important social issues it faces?

THE LAWS OF THE LAND

CLEVER AND UNRIGHTEOUS PEOPLE

DO PASS CLEVER AND UNJUST LAWS

FOR THEIR OWN SELFISH ENDS.

That the Bible never encourages sedition is abundantly clear. David, though twice given the opportunity to slay King Saul, wouldn't lay a hand on him. To David, whether or not Saul was a good king was immaterial. He was anointed and appointed by God. To ignore God's appointment would be to rebel against God's authority.

Jesus didn't lead a rebellion against Roman rule. Even from a human standpoint, considering the thousands that followed Him, He certainly could have. Instead, when accused, He didn't open His mouth to defend himself. He, an innocent man, died on a cross. Revolutionary? Inspiring? Yes. But not seditious.

Paul wrote, "Let every person be in subjection to the governing authorities. For there is no authority except from God, and those which exist are established by God" (Romans 13:1). When unjustly mistreated, he once responded (ignorantly) in a disrespectful way to his people's high priest. But when he discovered his error he replied, "I was not aware, brethren, that he was high priest; for it is written, 'You shall not speak evil of a ruler of your people'" (Acts 23:5).

LAW AND PREJUDICE

Nevertheless, we must never forget the devil's desire to control a nation (or any group) through its leaders. In the U.S., some in the judicial system have sought to replace the government's legislative branch in defining the laws by which we live. While laws are written by the legislature, they're not interpreted by those who wrote them as much as by those who enforce them—the judiciary. Thus we are now governed by an appointed judiciary and no longer exclusively by our elected officials.

At the highest levels, justices are appointed by the president, on whom special interest groups can have significant impact. Supreme Court justices tend to interpret the law according to the social bent that made them attractive candidates. As such, a justice appointed by a president with a particular social prejudice would tend toward that same prejudice in his or her rulings.

Both justice and injustice exist within the legal system. Where the laws of the land forbid free religious and moral rearing of children, the devil has effectively cut off the land's moral posterity. The next generation will have no social basis for morality. The moral fabric ensuring freedom and justice for all will unravel when people are no longer ruled by the law's spirit but by its letter.

"FREEDOM OF RELIGION AND CONSCIENCE"

Laws are often framed in ambiguous terms that permit arbitrary interpretation. This was precisely my (Michael's) concern as we read the new Russian laws passed on "freedom of religion and conscience" in 1997. As I considered the text, I noticed word choices. The articles allowed a broad legal interpretation within a specified range. In some cases the framers favored more ambiguous terms even when more precise terms were available. While the new laws didn't infringe on religious freedom, they did allow an arbitrary restriction of freedom. While the laws were not unjust, enforcement of them certainly could be.

Following Russia's lead, Central Asian republics began to consider similar legislation. Some elements considered as a result of Russia's laws:

(1) A religious organization must exist for at least fifteen years before it can register as a legal entity.
(2) Evangelization of anyone younger than eighteen is forbidden.
(3) Churches must provide the government with lists of their members.
(4) A panel of government-appointed secular experts would determine a religious group's legitimacy.
(5) The gospel could not be spread among other traditionally non-Christian ethnic groups.
(6) The government must approve leader appointments within "religious organizations."

Thankfully, due in large part to the prayers of the saints, some of these have yet to become law in Central Asia. However, the battle is far from over, and new restrictions threaten Christianity in both Russia and Central Asia.

CLEVER AND UNJUST LAWS

Clever and unrighteous people often pass clever and unjust laws for their own selfish ends. Legal battles against God's plans for His people are well organized and relentless. To illustrate: The United Nations General Assembly voted on 690 resolutions before 1990.

Almost two-thirds (429) were against Israeli interests. Of the 175 UN Security Council resolutions passed before 1990, more than half (97) were oppositional to Israel.

It is significant that while Israel represents a minute fraction of the world's landmass and population, the bulk of UN attention has been focused on it. Some would argue that these resolutions addressed legitimate grievances against the nation of Israel, but regardless, the main point is this: Satan often uses unrighteous people in high social and political positions to establish laws that restrict religious freedom. Vigilance is the price of liberty!

LAWS OF THE LAND: A FINAL WORD

Laws of the land are written and enforced by our leaders. In democratic societies, these leaders are elected. It's disgraceful that so few Christians participate in the voting process. While one person's vote may seem insignificant, like prayer, it's the cumulative effect that influences the legislature's composition, and this ultimately determines the man-made laws by which we live.

"Therefore to him that knoweth to do good, and doeth it not, to him it is sin" (James 4:17 KJV). Where Christians have the privilege to vote, they ought to vote. To neglect this privilege is to yield ground to the devil—it is sin. Leadership and laws are inextricably related. Your vote is an intercessory act. The prophet Samuel said, "God forbid that I should sin against the Lord in ceasing to pray for you" (1 Samuel 12:23 KJV).

How does the Lord see our failure to vote? At the very least, He must be displeased by our ambivalence and complacency. Voting is an act of intercessory vigilance. People who have a voice must use it if they wish to see change in people's lives. As cumulative prayer changes the hearts of men, the cumulative vote changes the leaders of nations.

APPLICATION

KEY POINTS

(1) Judges interpret and rule on the law according to the social bent that made them attractive candidates for their positions.

(2) Where the laws of the land forbid the free religious and moral upbringing of children, the devil has already effectively cut off the land's moral posterity.

(3) The moral fabric ensuring freedom and justice for all unravels when people are no longer ruled by the law's spirit but by its letter.

(4) Laws are often framed in ambiguous terms that permit arbitrary interpretation.

(5) Satan can and does use unrighteous people in high social and political positions to establish laws that restrict religious freedom.

(6) Since the laws of the land are written and enforced by our leaders, voting is an intercessory act whose cumulative effect will influence the legislature's composition, which will frame and pass the laws of the land by which we live.

SPIRITUAL RECONNAISSANCE

(1) What specific and significant changes of law (especially in regard to freedom of religion, conscience, or expression) has the government of our community recently enacted?

(2) In preparation for what repressive action might this law have been changed?

(3) Is there a legitimate and beneficent purpose behind this change in law?

(4) Are freedoms expanded or restricted by the new law?

(5) Who championed this law, and who opposed it?

(6) Why were they for or against this law, and what are their spiritual beliefs and priorities?

(7) Who are the judges in our region, and what are the legal issues they face for judgment?

(8) What is the apparent voting record of Christians in our community? Who are the Christian candidates in our community and for what offices are they running?

PERSONALIZE IT

(1) How do recent specific and significant changes of law (especially in regard to freedom of religion, conscience, or expression) affect me personally?

(2) How can these laws be used against me?

(3) How can these laws work in my favor?

(4) Are my freedoms expanded or restricted by the new law?

(5) How well do I personally know and relate to those who championed this law and to those who opposed it?

(6) Was I for or against this law? Why?

(7) Do I pray regularly for the judges appointed in my region and for the Christian resolution of the legal issues that face them for judgment?

(8) How seriously have I considered the Christian issues that will be influenced by my vote? How well do I know and relate to the Christian candidates in my community?

TARGET PHASING

THE SELECTION OF PRAYER TARGETS MUST PROCEED IN STRATEGIC PHASES.

There is a logical, God-ordained, spiritually strategic sequence in selecting prayer targets that provides optimal success. We discover this sequence by observing world circumstances and by listening to the Holy Spirit. Ignore the world's circumstances or the Spirit's voice and we're doomed to failure.

The Holy Spirit teaches us how to respond to changing circumstances, illuminating the principles behind successful strategies. Since He foresees future events, His sequencing of essential targets is unaffected by our wavering human will. Learning to lock in to His sequencing criteria enables us to hold steady against contrary winds. These criteria and the strategic initiatives they invoke are always governed by God-breathed, life-giving principles.

In discerning the Spirit's phasing of prayer targets, focus first on life, truth, and the Word of God. All His strategies confirm the Word, reveal truth, dismantle deception, and/or promote life. When asking the Spirit for His strategic sequencing, seek confirmation in God's Word. Ask what truth He's trying to reveal or what deception He's trying to dismantle. Look for the situation's life-giving aspects.

The Holy Spirit also knows the motives of men's hearts and is not fooled by how things appear. His phasing of events considers the inner motives that dictate action more than the actions themselves. The discerning of motives is dangerous ground, for we are to judge no one. But the fruit we see is an accurate indication of the motives employed, and we *are* enjoined to judge fruit. So when you have a check in your spirit, ask the Holy Spirit to reveal the true nature of fruit that looks good on the outside.

While watching coverage of the war on terror in Afghanistan, I (Michael) took note of the target phasing employed by the U.S. military. I realized that the sound, strategic principles it followed would also be useful in spiritual warfare prayer. Here (with my comments) are those phases as reported by the military.

Phase 1: "Clear the Air"

The first offensive action should be one that will most quickly degrade the enemy's ability to defend itself. In the above example, the U.S. needed first to minimize its own risk before it could confidently launch the offensive. This involved three main targets: (1) antiaircraft positions, (2) runways, and (3) aircraft.

To identify these targets, they employed surveillance methods, including satellites, high-altitude, pilotless drone aircraft, and visual ground target identification. They made their first pass with smart (laser-guided) weapons high enough to avoid antiaircraft fire but low enough to identify targets. Provoking the enemy response allowed them to immediately pinpoint and devastate enemy positions. Meanwhile, any massive enemy troop movements to establish or shore up defensive positions were easily monitored by satellite. These surveillance methods ensured that enemy troops would stay put and that every defensive response was met with a more accurate offensive response.

In a spiritual sense, here is one potential analogy (among many):

- ▸ "antiaircraft positions" are equivalent to *occult worship centers;*

- ▸ "runways" are their *indoctrination and training methods;*

- ▸ "aircraft" are the *individual occult figures* who aim to cause specific high-level damage.

To identify these targets we need intelligent intervention from our all-seeing Satellite (the Spirit of God), from drones (media and information sources), and from visual ground and high-altitude observers (local citizens and intercessory observers—for instance, the Observatory in Colorado Springs or the Sentinel Group of George Otis Jr.).

PHASE 2: "STRIKE MOBILIZATION CENTERS"

The war on terror in Afghanistan has involved two key types of mobilization centers: "command and control centers" and "armament centers" (ammunition dumps). Command and control centers provide strategic coordination of any military action. Armament centers act as staging areas and equip the troops with firepower and positioning to carry out strategic action. By striking and/or occupying these two types of centers, the U.S. created buffers against a coordinated, well-armed response to its military offensive.

Command and control centers regulate the flow of information, resources, and manpower. These may or may not be located in close proximity to a given center; their deployment, however, is the direct responsibility of these centers. Hence, the destruction of the enemy's key centers and the disruption of their activities are of primary importance.

In Afghanistan, the enemy's training camps across the country have represented the enemy's command and control centers. Among other things, they've provided recruitment, communication, training, assembly, and armament for the al-Qaeda terrorist network there.

In a spiritual sense, armament centers and command and control centers are spiritual power points, like temples to false gods or places of ritual worship that coordinate occult activity within a given geographic area (city, state, or nation). These centers typically tolerate all religious views except those that would depose them.

PHASE 3: "STRIKE STRATEGIC TROOP POSITIONS"

After neutralizing the air forces that could compromise their offensive, and after disarming future military campaigns and disrupting the communication that coordinated al-Qaeda's efforts, the U.S. proceeded to assault strategic and potentially threatening troop concentrations. They endeavored to dismantle and scatter the enemy's plans and initiatives by bombing front-line positions and by targeting key staging grounds (training camps) for impending military actions.

In the spiritual sense, by analogy, "strategic troop positions" represent the far-right and fanatically violent religious fundamentalists that breed unhealthy nationalism, violent religious intolerance, and hatred for anything that questions self-perceived superiority or infringes upon self-defined rights to position, statehood, wealth, or power.

What the U.S. will continue to do in Afghanistan remains to be seen. But we're confident they will build on their successes and learn from their failures (as will al-Qaeda). If we keep our eyes open, we too can learn from their successes and failures. This relates to prayer as follows:

(1) We must make a concerted effort to spiritually map the

capabilities of malicious spiritual forces—their capabilities to put our prayer warriors in harm's way or to render us incapable of achieving our prayer goals.

(2) We must focus concerted and consistent prayer on temple areas, places of ritual worship, and on behalf of those influenced by the spirits worshiped there.

(3) We must not shrink from assaulting in prayer those ideologies (and their demonic roots) that corrupt and demean our society.

PHASE 4: "GENUINE SURRENDER"

Before we leave this subject, we should consider a strategy the enemy regularly employs: "sabotaged surrender." True surrender is not an option for the devil. He won't surrender until he has no other choice. Accordingly, we must be careful not to confuse a strategic withdrawal with a genuine surrender. Retreat in order to regroup and return isn't surrender. The devil will feign "surrender" if he thinks it can catch us off guard and open a door for later sabotage. Thus, one of our target phases must be *genuine surrender*.

KEY POINTS

(1) There is a God-ordained, spiritually strategic sequence of prayer-target selection that will provide our best opportunity for success.

(2) To discover God's strategic prayer sequence, we must engage in Holy Spirit-directed reconnaissance.

(3) In discerning the Spirit's phasing of prayer targets, focus first on life, truth, and the Word of God.

(4) Strategic Phases:

    (a) *Phase 1: "Clear the Air"*—The first offensive action must be that which will most quickly degrade the enemy's ability to defend itself.

(b) *Phase 2: "Strike Mobilization Centers"*—the spiritual power points that coordinate occult activity within a geographic area (city, state, or nation).

(c) *Phase 3: "Strike Strategic Troop Concentrations"*—

  (i) We must apply concerted effort onto spiritually mapping the assault capabilities of spiritual forces—capabilities that could put our prayer warriors in harm's way or render us unable to achieve our prayer goals.

  (ii) We must focus concerted and consistent prayer toward temple areas and places of ritual worship and on behalf of those people influenced by the spirits worshipped there.

  (iii) We must not shrink back from assaulting in prayer those ideologies (and their demonic roots) that corrupt and demean our society.

(d) *Phase 4: "Genuine Surrender"*—true surrender is not an option for Satan, so do not mistake strategic withdrawal for genuine surrender. He will feign "surrender" if he thinks it will catch you off guard and open a door for later sabotage.

SPIRITUAL RECONNAISSANCE

(1) What territories or strategic abilities in our region is the enemy trying most to defend?

(2) What methods can we safely employ to identify those strategic targets?

(3) What should be our Christian community's immediate response to each target we identify?

(4) Where are the demonic "mobilization centers" in our community, and which ones coordinate and/or equip for action?

(5) What are the xenophobic, supremacist, or nationalistic groups in our community?

(6) What strategies does the enemy currently employ in our region to compromise the efforts of our prayer warriors?

(7) What ideologies in our community most corrupt or demean our society?

(8) Are there any issues of "unnatural surrender" in our community wherein the powers of darkness have seemingly conceded without a fight?

PERSONALIZE IT

(1) What areas or abilities in my life is the enemy trying most to defend?

(2) What methods can I safely employ to identify those strategic targets?

(3) What should be my immediate response to each target I identify?

(4) What are the demonic "mobilization centers" in my life, and how do they coordinate and/or equip demonic forces for action against me personally?

(5) What are my xenophobic (fear or hatred of strangers or foreigners), supremacist, or nationalistic tendencies?

(6) What strategies does the enemy currently employ in my life to compromise my prayer efforts?

(7) What ideologies in my mind most corrupt or demean my purpose in God?

(8) Are there any issues of "unnatural surrender" in my life wherein the powers of darkness have seemingly conceded without a fight?

TARGET MATCHING

EVERY TARGET MUST BE MATCHED
WITH THE MINIMUM FORCE NECESSARY
TO SUBDUE IT.

T o avoid wasting resources (time, people, and money) the U.S. military in Afghanistan chose weapons appropriate to the target they sought to destroy. Matching a target with appropriate strategic force, known in military circles as *weaponeering*, requires superb reconnaissance and careful consideration of each target as well as the corresponding capability of each weapon. After all, you can kill a fly with either a swatter or a sledgehammer.

FIRST-PRIORITY TARGETS

We also must prioritize and evaluate our prayer targets. If we don't have a system to do so, spiritual necessity requires that we develop one now. Millions of "Christian dollars" and much valuable Christian time are spent annually on prayer journeys that focus on low-priority targets. I'd also guess that much time, money, and effort is wasted on prayer journeys whose joint force or strategic impact is too spiritually feeble or ill-timed to have a significant effect on the chosen "major-force" or first-priority target. It's time for us to get as serious about prayer as we are about business, church growth, or military action. We mustn't allow negligence, apathy, or well-meaning distraction to rob God's kingdom of a generation of souls. We must not be robbed of the heavenly resources intended for us to use in reaching this generation for Christ.

MINIMUM NECESSARY FORCE

At Wagner Leadership Institute, in a class entitled *Spiritual Warfare: Power Encounters*, Professor Charles Kraft drives home the principle of target matching (weaponeering) in a practical way. Kraft emphasizes the importance of target matching in personal deliverance:

> Allegiance encounters confront and solve the problem of false allegiance. Truth encounters confront error and ignorance, while power encounters confront powers. You cannot confront power with truth. You can only confront power with another power and allegiance with another allegiance.

As previously stated, methods don't always work, but principles do. Therefore, if this is a reliable principle for ground level spiritual warfare (deliverance), it's reasonable for us to assume it can also be applied to strategic-level spiritual warfare. We must match the target with the minimum force necessary to subdue it. In this regard, we must also understand that prayer is an issue of power. The granting of spiritual power is an issue of allegiance. We are granted power and authority to use it based on our allegiance to the God of all truth.

It's time for us to involve ourselves wholeheartedly in *spiritual weaponeering*. God's economy will not favorably tolerate anything less. Let's not condone an unhealthy preoccupation with target analysis, which can rob us of what is most needed—well-informed, well-equipped *action*. But, failing to analyze our target will certainly cause unnecessary collateral damage both to God's kingdom and to the very people we are trying to rescue.

While avoiding unhealthy preoccupation with target analysis, we should adopt a healthy preoccupation with prayer. It is by the Spirit of God that we gain truly accurate spiritual insight into the strength and strategy of our spiritual opponent. Failure to pray will result in needless hardship and wasted time, money, and effort.

First-Deployment Forces

We must identify significant "major forces," first-priority prayer targets, and match them with the appropriate prayer force—*then* we mount our assaults at the appropriate and most significant time. This requires seasoned intercessors and skilled prophetic voices. We should enthusiastically engage them and adequately fund their participation in our efforts. They're no longer to be considered peripheral to the task; they are as central and strategic as first-deployment reconnaissance and assault forces.

The Evolutionary Nature of Warfare

Before moving on, we offer this word of caution. Throughout history, modes of warfare have experienced change. The combatants of each generation must adapt to new weapons and strategies in order to survive. Therefore, we must remember the evolutionary nature of war and keep current with its changing forms. Though warfare principles remain the same, the strategic exercise of those principles is constantly changing. We cannot fight today's advanced enemy with yesterday's antiquated ideas and weapons. We must be vigilant to perceive war's changing face and be prepared to change with it.

Our neglect of this caution will be apparent in the oppression and defeat we endure. *There are tools of the ages and tools of the age.* Tools of the ages include love, prayer, giving, and so forth. Spiritual mapping, for example, is a tool of the age, revealed to us in this generation for a reason.

As we've learned in the second Iraq war, a battle plan is in constant flux after the first shot. As combatants respond to one another, they discover each other's abilities and learn from their own mistakes. Error is a ruthless schoolmaster. The enemy knows this. He learns more from his mistakes than from his successes, and so must we. What won yesterday's war may not win a single battle tomorrow!

APPLICATION

KEY POINTS

(1) Target matching, aka "weaponeering," requires superb reconnaissance and careful consideration of each target and of the corresponding capability of each weapon.

(2) Familiarize yourself with God's first-priority prayer targets.

(3) The use of spiritual power is a privilege granted based on our allegiance to the God of all truth.

(4) Excessive target analysis can rob us of what is most needed—well-informed, well-equipped *action.*

(5) Negligence of target analysis will certainly cause unnecessary collateral damage both to God's kingdom and to the very people we're trying to help.

(6) Intercessors are strategic, first-deployment reconnaissance and assault forces.

(7) The combatants of each generation must remember the evolutionary nature of war and adapt to new weapons and strategies in order to survive.

(8) What won the war yesterday may not win a single battle tomorrow.

SPIRITUAL RECONNAISSANCE

(1) What are our community's first-priority prayer targets, the targets whose influence will most positively or negatively affect the whole community?

(2) What is the minimum necessary force that the Christian community must employ to bring about a positive change in each of these target areas?

(3) Which of these targets seem most neglected, and how is that neglect siphoning off our Christian resources?

(4) Who are our community's first-deployment forces, those whose prophetic and intercessory influence can have the most immediate and beneficial effect?

(5) What Christian strategies and weapons formerly employed against the forces of darkness in our region seem no longer to be effective?

PERSONALIZE IT

(1) What are my first-priority prayer targets, the targets whose influence will most positively or negatively affect my life and family?

(2) What is the minimum necessary force I must employ to bring about a positive change in each of these target areas?

(3) Which of these targets seem most neglected, and how is that neglect siphoning off my resources?

(4) Who are the first-deployment forces in my life, those whose prayerful and prophetic influence can have the most immediate and beneficial effect on the critical situations I face?

(5) What strategies and weapons I've formerly employed against the forces of darkness in my life seem no longer to be effective?

TIME-CRITICAL
TARGETING

PRAYER REVEALS TARGETS OF OPPORTUNITY
AND HELPS ORCHESTRATE THE TIME-CRITICAL
TARGETING THAT RESULTS
IN DELIVERANCE.

T he Bible is replete with examples of God's perfect timing. Consider, for instance, the story of Esther, the Jewish girl who came to a position of influence with the king *at the appropriate time* (Esther 2:15).

Esther's uncle, Mordecai, was standing in the gate to hear and reveal a plot against the king *at the appropriate time* (v. 22). Haman, chief adversary of the Jews, plotted to destroy Mordecai and all his kindred. Just as Haman was on his way to the king to suggest that Mordecai be hanged, the king asked, "What shall be done for the man whom the king delights to honor?" (6:6 NKJV).

Haman thought the king meant him (6:4–11). *At the appropriate time*, Esther revealed Haman's evil design against her and her people. After the king left in a rage, Haman, pleading for his life, threw himself across the couch where Esther lay. The king returned just in time to see him there and reply, "Will he also assault the queen while I am in the house?" (7:8 NKJV).

Haman was hanged on the very gallows he'd built for Mordecai. Few recognize the significance of this: *At the appropriate time*, after three days of prayer and fasting, these critical issues were decided. Fasting and prayer provided and orchestrated these time-critical targets of opportunity that resulted in the salvation of the Jews.

THE APPROPRIATE TIME

Targets are timing-critical. There is always an appropriate, strategic time for focusing on any target. Focusing on a target too late will allow that target to gain an advantage over you. Focusing on a target too soon won't fulfill the desired strategic results.

This principle is abundantly clear in military conflict. Those responsible for target selection must consider how immediate a threat the target poses, the potential for collateral damage, and whether or not hitting the target now would achieve the desired result.

Take, for example, the targeting of a military installation. What's the most opportune time for a strike? Perhaps early enough to hinder construction before time, money, and resources have been poured in. But an even more strategic time would be when the target is nearly finished but not yet operational. The "finished but not yet operational" stage is the optimal strike stage because it robs the enemy of his resources *and* his operational threat.

Optimum time for a strike also means the time requiring optimum vigilance. Satan, a master of this strategy, is aggressive and vigilant at critical times. The good news is that he always overplays his hand, and he usually ends up shooting himself in the foot.

Regarding our target selection in the spirit world, discernment of timing-critical issues is vital to our success. Too often in our selection we are more reactionary than visionary. We tend to wait until catastrophe has already struck before praying for a certain person or situation. We must learn to spiritually discern the significance of individuals and events and pray for them with prophetic anticipation. We must discern the immediacy of the threats we face personally, locally, regionally, nationally, and internationally.

When and how we pray is of paramount importance. We must strike the prayer target posing the greatest threat with surgical precision at precisely the right time. Failure to consider the timing and the minimum necessary force to neutralize the target can produce disastrous and sometimes irreversible results. Whole governments and entire movements can hang in the balance of our prayer timing and finesse. How, when, and for what we pray should be Spirit-directed and never slipshod or reactionary.

When a target has been identified and the timing for a strike has been discerned, then it's necessary to accurately assess the *minimum necessary force* required to destroy the target. We call this force "finesse." A ten-million-dollar weapon isn't needed to destroy a two-dollar target. As President George W. Bush is reported to so eloquently have stated, "When I take action, I'm not going to fire a $2 million missile at a $10 empty tent and hit a camel in the butt. It's going to be decisive" (*Newsweek*, 9/24/01). In the long run, regardless of the effort's cost, good reconnaissance always pays for itself.

Discerning the most immediate threats from the broad range of potentially harmful targets means *we need spiritual reconnaissance*. That is to say, we need people with open minds and open hearts who can hear what the Spirit of God is saying to the churches. These special-operations reconnaissance experts are the intercessors and prophets the Lord has dispersed throughout the worldwide body of Christ. There's no nation in which these individuals do not exist. However, many in the body often don't recognize their importance, and they themselves frequently don't recognize the prophetic and intercessory gifts latent within them. Accordingly, one strategic and timing-critical target is to pray that in every nation prophets and intercessors would rise to their calling and be recognized by the body of Christ. Without these specialists, our targeting will be out of focus, ill-timed, and ineffective.

In military conflict, the special-ops forces alert Central Command to the sequence, timing, placement, and intensity of strategic strikes. In both defensive and offensive postures, failure to obtain this information can spell disaster. We would do well to employ that principle in spiritual warfare.

TARGETS OF OPPORTUNITY

In March 2003, Operation Iraqi Freedom was almost over before it began. By mobilizing a strike against a "target of opportunity," coalition forces severely hampered the strategic interests of the advancing Iraqi military. Superb intelligence identified key enemy leaders as being in a single place at a strategic time. To strike this group, in this place, at this time required troop and leadership flexibility; it represented the greatest strategic hope for minimizing casualties and for shortening the length and intensity of military engagement.

That principle also should be applied in spiritual warfare. There are key gatherings of significant leaders that we should know about and pray over. When the devil has control over these gatherings, they represent evil's decision-making apparatus. The decisions made will potentially influence millions of souls for eternity. Such targets of opportunity must not be missed.

Timing-critical prayer targeting depends on discernment. Discernment depends on sensitivity to the Holy Spirit. Sensitivity to the Holy Spirit is the hallmark of intercessors and prophets, God's special-ops forces. And they must exercise caution.

DIAGNOSIS DOESN'T MEAN ASSIGNMENT

The following is an account from Alice Smith.

Eddie and I helped start a church in the fall of 1982, in Houston, Texas. While researching Houston, we uncovered some strategic historical information about how territorial spirits had gained legal right to our city. So in the winter of 1983, I was praying for Houston, and day after day I asked the Lord to show me the territorial spirits over it. Finally, with an air of confidence, after about six weeks, I felt God had given me the names of the principalities of Houston. Zealously, I began to attack and blast them through warfare prayer by saying, "You spirit of death, get out of my city. We don't want you here. I stand against your every scheme to steal, kill, and destroy."

After several weeks of attacking the devil, I came dangerously close to death. I developed an infection from a gall bladder attack and came within twelve hours of dying from peritonitis of the spleen and liver. Within fourteen months, I had almost destroyed my family. Eddie and I had six surgeries, three of them not covered by insurance. We had depleted $35,000 in savings and were on the brink of losing our home. With a growing family, a new baby, and an eighteen-month-old church that had just lost its first senior pastor, I was close to "giving up in the road." The church was struggling, we were struggling, and the enemy was laughing. I was experiencing what some call "the dark night of the soul."

After our situation settled, about fifteen months later, I asked the Lord about this. He spoke into my heart clearly. *Alice, I told you the names of the spirits over Houston, but you didn't ask me what to do with the revelation.* I couldn't believe it! Now I know. We have authority to deal with the enemy, but our authority is ambassadorial. The Lord's time and instruction are absolutely crucial in the fight. I was fighting the battle on my own without His direction. I learned that just because we have a diagnosis doesn't mean God has given us an assignment. I repented for this, and it was a costly lesson to learn. (*Power Praying*, 1998)

KEY POINTS

(1) All targets are timing-critical and have an appropriate time for our attention.
(2) The optimal-strike stage is also the time requiring optimum vigilance.
(3) Pray proactively, being more visionary than reactionary, by praying with prophetic anticipation for individuals and events.
(4) Governments and movements hang in the balance of intercessory prayer timing and finesse.
(5) In every nation, there are prophets and intercessors who have yet to rise to their special-ops calling of alerting the body of Christ to the sequence, timing, placement, and intensity of strategic forces.
(6) Without the help of these spiritual-reconnaissance experts, our prayer targeting will remain unfocused, ill-timed, and ineffective.

SPIRITUAL RECONNAISSANCE

(1) What Christian ministries or projects seem to be at an optimal-strike stage and therefore require heightened vigilance?
(2) Do the prayers of our Christian leaders seem more consistently visionary or reactionary?
(3) What is the minimum force necessary to protect or decimate each optimal target we've identified?
(4) Who are the Christians in our community with open hearts and minds that are able to hear what God's Spirit is currently saying to our churches?
(5) What are the gatherings of significant leaders that we should

consider as targets of opportunity and therefore pray over most intensely?

PERSONALIZE IT

(1) Which of my ministries or projects seem to be at an optimal-strike stage and thus require heightened prayer vigilance?

(2) Which of my consistent prayers are more visionary, and which are more reactionary?

(3) What is the minimum force necessary to protect or decimate each optimal target I've identified?

(4) Who are the Christians in my life with open hearts and minds that are able to hear and confirm what God's Spirit may be currently saying to me?

(5) What are the gatherings of significant family members or community leaders that I should consider as targets of opportunity and thus pray over most intensely?

THE PRIORITY QUADRANT

AS SPIRITUAL CIRCUMSTANCES CHANGE, THE
INTERCESSOR MUST REMAIN SUFFICIENTLY
ALERT, SENSITIVE, AND DISCERNING TO
RESPOND AND PRIORITIZE PRAYERS.

A useful tool to facilitate target phasing, target matching (weaponeering), and time-critical targeting is the priority quadrant on the next page. Along with the Holy Spirit's leading, this can help you identify and process truly mission-critical information. We don't know its origin, but it's helpful in prioritizing just about anything.

The quadrant basically has two axes. The vertical axis measures the *impact*, on a scale of zero to ten, with ten signifying the most impact an action will have on one or more individuals. The horizontal axis measures the *urgency*, on a scale of zero to ten, with ten being the most urgent.

By cross-referencing your perspective of an action's *impact* and *urgency*, the action will fall into one of four blocks.

▸ *High Impact/High Urgency:* Actions in this block are your greatest priorities.

▸ *Low Impact/Low Urgency:* Actions in this block are your lowest priorities.

▸ Actions that fall into either of the other two blocks can be prioritized according to the highest value an action may hold on either axis.

▸ If something has a 5/5 value, it should appear in the middle of your priority list.

▸ Likewise, actions with a 10/10 value are top priority; actions with a 0/0 value are bottom priority.

High Impact High Urgency						High Impact Low Urgency				
					10					
					9					
					8					
					7					
					6					
10	9	8	7	6	5	4	3	2	1	0
					4					
					3					
					2					
Low Impact High Urgency					1	Low Impact Low Urgency				
					0					

In the same way this scale is used to prioritize actions it can also be used to prioritize prayers. However, one thing to remember: Prayers are not always as static in their values as are actions. The dynamic values of prayers change the physical world more quickly and often more subtly than the values of actions. *Actions primarily influence the physical world with secondary spiritual consequences; prayers primarily influence the spirit world with secondary physical consequences.* As spiritual circumstances change, the intercessor must remain alert, sensitive, and discerning enough to respond accordingly.

This spiritual fluidity or flexibility can't be taught in a classroom. You may find ways to measure what you did right or wrong, but that knowledge will remain theoretical until you begin to pray. Prayer must be learned by experience and practice. The golfer improves his swing by swinging. The flyer improves his flight by flying. The intercessor hones his skill by praying. There are no training films you can watch to improve your "spiritual swing." The only way to hone the spiritual ability required to pray the right prayer at the right time is to pray.

Finally, in target phasing, target matching, and time-critical targeting, recall that the appropriate prayer must be prayed with the appropriate force, at the appropriate time, in order to achieve the desired results. Personal prayer to pull down all the strongholds of Satan is not likely to have the impact that corporate prayer would have. Such presumption may even endanger the novice intercessor. Likewise, not every personal prayer requires a massive corporate force. Strategic time and strategic force must be applied to see strategic results.

KEY POINTS

(1) Prayers are not as static as actions and must be prioritized differently.

(2) Actions primarily influence the material realm with secondary spiritual consequences.

(3) Prayers primarily influence the spiritual realm with secondary material consequences.

(4) The mechanics of spiritual sensitivity must be learned through experience.

High Impact High Urgency					10 9 8 7 6	High Impact Low Urgency				
10	9	8	7	6	5	4	3	2	1	0
Low Impact High Urgency					4 3 2 1 0	Low Impact Low Urgency				

SPIRITUAL RECONNAISSANCE

(1) What corporate prayers do you believe will have the most impact on the greatest number of people? (In the world? In your nation? In your state? In your city?)

(2) What corporate prayers do you believe are most urgent? (For the world? For your nation? For your state? For your city?)

(3) List your 10/10 prayers for world, nation, state, and city, and compare them with the lists of other intercessors.

(4) Who would you involve in praying these 10/10 prayers?

(5) Other than prayer, what's the first step you must take to motivate their participation?

PERSONALIZE IT

(1) What personal prayers do you believe will have the most impact on you and on the greatest number of friends, relatives, and family members?

(2) Who will be the most directly impacted by these prayers?

(3) What personal prayers do you believe are most urgent?

(4) What makes them urgent?

(5) List your 10/10 prayers for yourself, for your family, for your relatives, for your friends, and for your neighborhood. Then ask your
cell leader or another Christian friend to agree with you in prayer
for these 10/10 requests.

PART 3

THE BATTLEGROUND OF THE MIND

CULTURAL
WORLDVIEWS

A WORLDVIEW IS NOT SOMETHING YOU'RE
BORN WITH. IT GROWS AND DEVELOPS AS YOU
GROW IN KNOWLEDGE AND EXPERIENCE LIFE.
KNOWLEDGE THAT CORRESPONDS WITH YOUR
EXPERIENCE IS ACCEPTED INTO YOUR
WORLDVIEW. KNOWLEDGE THAT CONTRADICTS
YOUR EXPERIENCE OR YOUR CURRENT
WORLDVIEW IS REJECTED.

As I (Michael) sat on the carpet, chewing my first bite of roasted baby camel, I began to understand what a different world I had entered. So much was unfamiliar. With pride, this Bedouin family had pointed out the new door they'd hung in honor of their guest, Dr. M. (Apparently doors are a status symbol found only in their cities.) Now in a high-walled room with one window near the ceiling, we sat close to the floor where it was cool. We were provided with cushions to recline on or to set against the wall behind us. *What a remarkable experience*, I thought. *Led into the desert by a truckload of Bedouin in a white Toyota.* Except for the truck, I felt as if I'd stepped out of the twenty-first century.

I hadn't seen a single woman since I'd arrived. Though I knew they'd prepared the food, two men carried it in and served us on a low banquet table packed with an abundance of delicacies I'd never seen before. The smells were foreign, and no eating utensils were to be found—I knew I was about to break one of my mother's household rules and eat with my hands. For this special occasion, our hosts had bought bottled soft drinks and with great ceremony had placed them on the table and poured our glasses full. They gave us their best, and it was bountiful and delicious.

When it was time to eat, though everyone was hungry, no one moved to the table presumptuously. Instead, the family elder, whom Dr. M. had seen healed several weeks earlier, motioned to each of us, directing where we should sit. First, the guest of honor was to sit directly across from the old man. Next, the man's two eldest sons sat on his right and his left. Then, placing the other guests with a wave of his hand, he indicated that the rest of the men could sit wherever they liked. Though the setting, the food, and the process were unfamiliar to me, I knew that to them any contrary arrangement would be abnormal.

Two Battlegrounds

You were not born with your worldview, which grows and develops as you grow in knowledge and experience life. You accept into your worldview knowledge that corresponds with your experience. You reject knowledge that contradicts your experience or your current worldview. From this perspective, there are two battlegrounds the devil craves to possess: *experience* and *knowledge*. Satan is desperately trying to interfere in these two areas of your life. If he can corrupt your experience, he can corrupt your worldview. Where you lack experience, he can corrupt your knowledge.

INFORMATION DIET

Knowledge is nothing more than information. A person's worldview is built in part on the information he's fed. If he's fed a healthy, balanced information diet, he will develop a healthy, balanced worldview; if he's fed an unbalanced information diet, he will develop an unbalanced worldview. If overfed on information, he'll be unable to properly process what he receives, and his worldview will be encumbered with unnecessary info. If information-starved, his worldview will be weak and debilitated. *A person's worldview reflects his information diet.*

PROPAGANDA DIET

Like candy, propaganda, no matter how good it tastes, has no nutritional soul-value. Propaganda is a one-sided information presentation, designed to elicit a specific response for the benefit of the presenter. Though it may incorporate truth, because it intentionally arranges or spins info to create a distorted view of reality, propaganda, on the whole, is hopelessly flawed and wholly unhealthy. The eventual result of a propaganda diet is a weak, debilitated, dependent soul. Propaganda corrupts a person's worldview.

When truth hangs in the balance, worldview will tip the scale for or against it. As we've seen, a person offered only one view has no alternative but to accept it as true. This isn't an intrinsic problem if the view is true—truth is healthy, and a person afforded accurate and true perspectives would have an excellent opportunity to form a healthy worldview. But if the view is false or incomplete, the observer will act in ways that may be harmful to himself and others. False information forms and feeds false conclusions.

Deception by propaganda, the oldest demonic tactic known to

man, dates back to when Satan fed Eve false and misleading information (propaganda). Essentially, he corrupted her worldview and minimized his efforts to tempt Adam. Without Eve's help, Adam may have been more difficult to deceive (see 1 Timothy 2:14). By distorting Eve's worldview, Satan was able to enlist her help in tempting Adam to sin. If the devil can fool us into believing his worldview, we will naturally do his work instead of engaging in God's.

WORLDVIEW DNA MARKERS

Worldviews are spiritual DNA markers. Worldviews become evident:

▸ *During times of crisis.* By observing how a culture reacts to crisis you can identify life-and-death worldview strongholds that dominate the culture's thinking.

▸ *In rites of transition.* By analyzing a culture's observance of transition rites (such as birth, circumcision, marriage, and death) you can identify how a worldview is propagated within the culture.

▸ *Through proverbs and myths.* By analyzing proverbs you can discover the pillars of wisdom upon which a worldview is based and accepted. By analyzing myths you can discover the origin of worldviews.

▸ *By contrasting differing cultural perceptions.* By contrasting how different cultures perceive common actions (such as holding hands, eating, or greeting others) you can discover how the culture's worldview is acted out in daily life.

▸ *Through analyzing how words are categorized within a language.* By studying word categorization you can learn how ideas are formed and why certain ideas are unimaginable within that culture.

These discoveries that help us build a culture map are important to our selection of strategic prayer targets. Without this information, our targeting will be weak and ineffective. If we take time to carefully observe the worldview of the culture we're trying to reach with the gospel, our prayers and efforts will be considerably more accurate, more comprehensive, and more fruitful.

APPLICATION

KEY POINTS

(1) Experience and knowledge are battlegrounds the devil craves to possess.

(2) Knowledge is nothing more than information.

(3) A person's worldview reflects his information diet.

(4) Propaganda corrupts a person's worldview.

(5) With truth in the balance, a person's worldview tips the scale for or against it.

(6) A person offered only one view has no alternative but to accept it as true.

(7) If the devil can fool us into believing his worldview, we will naturally do his work instead of engaging in the works of God.

(8) Worldviews become evident during times of crisis, in rites of transition, through proverbs and myths, by contrast of differing cultural perceptions, and by analyzing how words are categorized within a language. Each of these is a worldview DNA marker.

SPIRITUAL RECONNAISSANCE

(1) In what areas has the devil corrupted the communal experience, and thereby the worldview, of our community?

(2) In what areas has a lack of communal experience seemed to facilitate a communal lack of knowledge?

(3) Does it appear that the general information flow in our community is (a) limited, (b) normal, or (c) excessive?

(4) Does there seem to be a specific "propaganda diet" consistently fed into our community?

(5) What are the worldview DNA markers indicated by how our community reacts to crisis and transition? What worldview markers are indicated by our colloquial use of language? (See Key Point 8, above.)

PERSONALIZE IT

(1) In what areas has the devil corrupted my experience and thereby my worldview?

(2) In what areas has my lack of experience seemed to facilitate my lack of knowledge?

(3) Does it appear that the general information flow in my life is (a) limited, (b) normal, or (c) excessive?

(4) Does there seem to be a specific "propaganda diet" I am being consistently fed?

(5) What are my worldview DNA markers—indicated by how I react to crisis and transition? What worldview markers are indicated by my use of language? (See Key Point 8, above.)

POLITICAL WORLDVIEWS

IT IS FAR MORE PRUDENT FOR
CORRUPT LEADERS TO DENY THE TRUTH THAN
TO ADMIT THE TRUTH THAT
WOULD DEPOSE THEM.

Some nations have political philosophies that deny the existence of an unprejudiced God. Allowing for a loving and just God would force a change in government. While benefiting people in general, such an overhaul would force accountability, expose corruption, and rob leaders of personal wealth and power. Clearly, it's far more prudent for corrupt leaders to deny the truth than to admit the truth that would depose them. To them, anything is preferable to admitting the existence of the One True God, intimately involved in the affairs of men, who will one day judge the living and the dead.

THREE PREDOMINANT WORLDVIEWS

There are three predominant worldviews that must be opposed by all who love the truth. These correspond to three of the world's major religious blocs.

▶ *Humanism* says there is no God. We are the fabrication of chance in a random and meaningless universe. Humanism is exalted prominently through communism.

▶ *Traditionalism* maintains that there is a God but he's far too remote to be concerned with trivial human matters. Traditionalism is expressed clearly in organized religions that exalt tradition above human life.

▶ *Animism* teaches that many gods must be served devotedly in order to appease their insatiable appetites and to calm their angry and vengeful personalities. Animism is expressed commonly within folk religions.

Surprisingly, these three worldviews are not mutually exclusive—they frequently intermingle. There seems to be no contradiction in principle that forbids them from exchanging ideas or practices. By contrast, true Christianity gives no place to ideas or practices that minimize the value of people or their relationship with the loving and just God who created them.

WORLDVIEW FILTER

Like a defeated boxer breathlessly trying to survive to the next round, the devil sometimes minimizes his effort in order to conserve his resources for survival. He minimizes his efforts by promoting skewed worldviews. What he doesn't quite understand is that the fight truly is over, and he's lost. Though the bell has already rung, Satan now pounds the air and assaults the spectators, though they are powerless to change the outcome.

A person's worldview is his default setting. When he's confronted with new information, it's automatically run through his default "worldview filter" for interpretation. If his worldview is skewed, his interpretation of the new info will be wrong, resulting in error. Error can be fatal.

When we pray, we are seeking to minimize the devil's demented and delusional efforts. We do this by praying for truth to expose and overcome traditions and lies that cause leaders to form and act on distorted worldviews. As we pray against worldviews that exclude God's existence or malign His character, we must pray on behalf of those leaders who by virtue of their position promote them. We *must* pray for these leaders!

(1) Pray that they would love truth and righteousness.
(2) Pray that God will open their eyes to eternal realities and the consequences of their actions.
(3) Pray that God will reveal His love for them, that they'll come to know it and share it with others.

We must also pray for the disintegration of any systems that support corrupt worldviews and against the spiritual principalities that promote them. Through the knowledge of God's Word, we must immunize ourselves and our communities against political-deception infections. Above all, through study and practical application of the Word, we must remain champions of truth.

APPLICATION

KEY POINTS

(1) Three predominant worldviews must be *opposed* by all truth-lovers.
(a) That there is no God, and that we are the fabrication of chance in a random and meaningless universe
(b) That there is a God but that he's too remote to be

concerned about mankind.

(c) That there are many gods who must be served devotedly in order to appease their insatiable appetites and calm their angry and vengeful personalities.

(2) These worldviews correspond with three of the world's major religious blocs: humanism, traditionalism, and animism.

(3) The devil works to corrupt worldviews because, like a desperate and defeated fighter, he must minimize effort in order to conserve resources.

(4) We must pray for the disintegration of systems that support corrupt worldviews and against the spiritual principalities that promote them.

(5) Through practical knowledge of the Word, we can immunize ourselves and our communities against political-deception infections.

SPIRITUAL RECONNAISSANCE

(1) Which of the three predominant worldviews seems most prominent in our region?

(2) How does this worldview skew the interpretation of information that people here are receiving?

(3) Which of our community leaders seem most influenced by this world-view, and how do their actions reflect their beliefs?

(4) How might we share with these leaders in such a way that they can discover the truth for themselves without our damaging their dignity?

(5) How can we use God's Word to immunize ourselves against the specific effects of this negative worldview?

PERSONALIZE IT

(1) Which of the three predominant worldviews seems most prominent in my life?

(2) How does it skew the interpretation of information I am receiving?

(3) Which areas in my life seem most influenced by this worldview, and how do my actions reflect my beliefs in these areas?

(4) Who can help me discover the truth for myself without damaging my self-esteem?

(5) How can I use God's Word to immunize myself against the specific effects of this negative worldview?

THE SPIRIT OF TRUTH

INTERCESSION IS FAR MORE THAN PRAYER.
INTERCESSION IS ALSO SALTING OUR
CONVERSATION WITH THE WORD OF TRUTH.

I will ask the Father, and he will give you another Counselor to be with you forever—the Spirit of truth. The world cannot accept him, because it neither sees him nor knows him. But you know him, for he lives with you and will be in you. (John 14:16–17 NIV)

The Holy Spirit (often called the Spirit of Truth), given by the Father at the request of His Son, is a Counselor. He is to be our intimate companion, living not only *with* us but actually *in* us—*forever*. By God's grace we can see Him and know Him. But the world, because it neither sees nor knows Him, cannot accept Him. Therefore, when we speak by the Spirit of God, the world *cannot* recognize our words as truth. So when the world rejects us, they are not rejecting us but the One dwelling in us through whom we speak. As intercessors, our battle is to break through the world's wall of resistance to the Spirit of Truth. But how?

THE TESTIMONY
OF JESUS

When the Counselor comes, whom I will send to you from the Father, the Spirit of truth who goes out from the Father, he will testify about me. (John 15:26 NIV)

Our first offensive weapon against the world's wall of resistance is the double-edged sword of the Spirit. With one stroke of revelation, one edge awakens our own hearts to the truth of what we say about Him. With the same stroke, the other edge awakens the hearts of our listeners as we testify about our Lord. It's the work of the Spirit to awaken hearts to God's Word, but it's our work to preach the Word that the Spirit uses. Intercession is far more than prayer. Intercession is also salting our conversation with the Word of truth. Declaring God's Word in everyday conversation is a form of intercession that breaks down resistance to the truth.

Clarification: We're not referring to slinging religious jargon or trite clichés. No one is edified by that, especially the lost. We're referring to speaking truth and dispensing godly wisdom in our daily lives.

ALL TRUTH

When He, the Spirit of truth, comes, he will guide you into all truth. He will not speak on his own; he will speak only what he hears, and he will tell you what is yet to come. (John 16:13 NIV)

The Spirit of Truth is grieved with our partial, incomplete knowledge of truth. He wants our knowledge to be comprehensive.

He will guide us into *all* truth and give us *all* the information necessary to ensure our understanding of truth and the accuracy of our prayers (see 2 Peter 1:2–4).

In contrast, Satan (the father of lies) limits the information we receive, offering us only enough to encourage us to draw false conclusions. It's imperative that we recognize this fundamental difference between the Spirit of Truth and the spirit of lies.

There are other differences that also help us to discern truth and to pray more accurately. The Spirit of Truth doesn't speak for himself; He's accountable to God the Father. He doesn't spew forth empty or harmful words but speaks only beneficent words ordained by the Father. The spirit of lies, on the other hand, speaks maliciously, without restraint, from his own wicked heart. He refuses to be accountable to God.

Finally, the Spirit of Truth warns us of what is to come, while the spirit of lies enshrouds the future in a cloak of dark and terrifying mystery.

DISCOVERING THE SPIRIT OF TRUTH

We are from God, and whoever knows God listens to us; but whoever is not from God does not listen to us. This is how we recognize the Spirit of truth and the spirit of falsehood. (1 John 4:6 NIV)

We also discern truth by observing how others react upon hearing it. While those *not* from God won't and cannot listen to the truth, those who *are* of God love the truth. They hunger and thirst for it. They seek it.

This too is how we recognize the Spirit of Truth and the spirit of lies. Lovers of falsehood look for lies to conceal their dark deeds. They thirst for the ungodly agreement that will massage their seared consciences. They tenaciously guard the mask that expresses the false and flawless image they want the world to see. Lovers of truth seek to get and give the knowledge that will enable them and others to live true, holy, pure, and genuine lives in the sight of God and man.

We can pray hand in hand with our most powerful ally, the Spirit of Truth. Prayer in any other spirit will only produce pain and deception. As we intercede, we must make room for the Spirit in our daily conversation. As we engage in spiritual warfare against our malicious and ruthless foe, the Spirit must have preeminence in our lives. Prayer in the Spirit of Truth will destroy demonic strongholds, open blind eyes, and release captives. We can't go wrong by praying for revelation of the truth. Truth is at the center of every strategic prayer target!

APPLICATION

KEY POINTS

(1) The Spirit of Truth wants to be our intimate companion, living not only *with* us but actually living *in* us—*forever.*

(2) It's the work of the Spirit to awaken hearts to God's Word, but it's the work of believers to preach the Word of truth that the Spirit uses.

(3) Declaring God's Word in everyday conversation is a form of intercession that breaks down resistance to the truth.

(4) The Spirit of Truth is never satisfied with our partial or incomplete knowledge of truth; the spirit of falsehood limits the information we receive, granting us only enough to encourage inaccurate conclusions.

(5) The Spirit of Truth does not speak on His own but is accountable to God; the spirit of falsehood speaks maliciously from his own wicked heart without restraint or accountability to God.

(6) The Spirit of Truth warns us of what is to come; the spirit of falsehood enshrouds the future in a cloak of dark and terrifying mystery.

(7) We discern truth by observing how others react to those who speak it.
(8) In your prayers, you cannot go wrong by praying for revelation of the truth.
(9) Truth is at the center of every strategic prayer target!

SPIRITUAL RECONNAISSANCE

(1) In what areas of our community does there seem to be a spiritual wall of resistance built up against the Spirit of Truth?
(2) Which groups seem to react most vehemently against the public or private mention of the name of Jesus Christ or of the truth He represents?
(3) In what areas and over what issues does it seem that information in our community is most limited, corrupted, or repressed?
(4) What local lies of the enemy serve to obscure or minimize the severity of communal sins?

PERSONALIZE IT

(1) In what areas in my life does there seem to be a spiritual wall of resistance built up against the Spirit of Truth?
(2) In which areas do I seem to react most vehemently against the public or private mention of the name of Jesus Christ or of the truth He represents?
(3) In what areas and over what issues does it seem that information in my life is most limited, corrupted, or repressed?
(4) What lies of the enemy serve to obscure or minimize the severity of my sins?

COMPLAINING AND DISCONTENT

COMPLAINTS ARE LITTLE "GODS" THAT WE
BUILD IN OUR OWN IMAGE.

[Do not] grumble, as some of them did, and were destroyed by the destroyer. (1 Corinthians 10:10)

We (Michael and Aimee) had recently moved into our dream house in Merida, Venezuela. From our home, nestled along the jungle road just past the banana, citrus, and mango trees on the mountainside, we could see the snow-covered peak of Mount Bolivar. Truthfully, not everything had been idyllic since the move—great location, but we had encountered some problems.

All but one of the chicks we'd bought (to lay eggs, hopefully) turned out to be roosters. I'd built them a pen and dug a garden for them to scratch around in, and now I was suffering from unexplainable back pain. The X rays revealed nothing and all tests were inconclusive. When I mentioned to the doctor that it was only spiritual warfare, he suggested to Aimee that perhaps I wasn't "playing with a full deck." However, my physical situation was so severe she had to help dress me every morning.

Our neighbors regularly stole anything they could get their hands on—strawberry plants, bird feeders, even Aimee's dishwashing sponge, drying in the kitchen window.

Sometime back, a colony of ants had moved into the house in the middle of the night. The next morning we discovered an ant trail from the front door to our living room linen closet. The closet walls were literally crawling with this black mass, carrying eggs and setting up camp. (Praise God for insect spray.)

Elsewhere in the house, we regularly saw scorpions, especially coming from the shower drain. Every night we performed a bed check. And from that point we always shook out our shoes before putting them on.

Now, not surprisingly, we were again without water. In the past three months we'd had running water for only a few weeks. Our direct source was a mountain stream five kilometers away, and someone kept stealing the feeder pipe.

When the water eventually returned to the system and remained for two straight weeks, I went down the mountain to congratulate the community president. "Did you catch the thief?" I asked.

"Yes," he replied.

"Did you put him in jail?"

"Not exactly. We are paying him to guard the pipe."

The poor man just needed money to provide for his family.

In addition to the lack of water, we had neither money nor food. It was at this time that the Lord spoke to my wife to think of one good thing each day for which to be thankful and to be thankful for that one thing all day long. Under our circumstances we began to understand that discouragement, division, and distraction were weapons of the devil. To avoid succumbing to his attack, we knew we must avoid all complaining, criticism, and confusion about our call.

I remember that day well. I'd determined in my heart that, despite the pain, I would praise the Lord. In my morning devotion, I forced myself to dance before Him. Aimee had determined in her heart that regardless of the circumstances she would be thankful. That morning the Lord prompted her to write a list, by faith, of all the groceries she would buy *if* she had the money.

In the afternoon we had an unexpected visit from Mr. and Mrs. Hunt, an amazing missionary couple who after twenty-eight years on the field still had remarkable compassion for people. Eugene was tall and thin with a wry humor. Mary Olive was short and plump, and love oozed from her like melting butter.

She walked into our kitchen with a box full of groceries that held everything on Aimee's list plus a few things she'd forgotten. "I woke up this morning and I just began to pray for you," she said as she set the box on our table, "and the Lord just said to buy you these groceries and pay you a little visit. So here we are. I hope you can use everything." As we received the much-needed provisions I felt amply rewarded for refusing to complain and for keeping the right attitude in the midst of our trials. We had all we needed. What joy!

YIELD OR CONQUER

Death and slavery are the best of friends; the one comes when we succumb to the other (Romans 6:16). Slavery comes when we fear conflict. Battle is the price of victory, and victory is the price of freedom. *When encountering a conflict, we really only have two choices: yield or conquer.* If we do not conquer, by default we yield. There can be no compromise with the devil.

Complaining is yielding to and confessing our fear of defeat. When we rehearse our fears, like an oft-repeated story, the villain looms larger and larger in our own minds with each telling. Complaining compromises our faith in God and feeds our fear and discouragement. Fear and complaint suffocate our potential for victory. We must be careful not to rehearse our fears in our prayers. Our prayer targets must reflect our faith in God and the victories He's already won. Don't use your prayers to whine against Him! Complaints are little "gods" we create in our own minds.

Complaining feeds discontent. Discontent breeds revolution. The intercessor must understand that wherever he hears consistent complaining, in that sphere, discontent and revolution are not far behind. In Soviet Russia, the Bolsheviks bred discontent in preparation for their revolt. They couldn't oppose the czar publicly, so instead they formed "home groups" that aired their grievances with the government in a confidential setting. This was not unlike the activity of Absalom, who stood in the gates and stole the hearts of the men of Israel.

PUTTING GOD TO THE TEST

When Moses delayed his coming down from Mount Sinai, the people complained to Aaron, wanting him to fashion a god for them. And, at Hazeroth, Miriam complained against Moses' Ethiopian wife. Finally, after the Israelites spied out Canaan and whined about "giants in the land," God declared,

> *Because all these men who have seen My glory and the signs which I did in Egypt and in the wilderness, and have put Me to the test now these ten times, and have not heeded My voice, they certainly shall not see the land of which I swore to their fathers, nor shall any of those who rejected Me see it.* (Numbers 14:22–23 NKJV)

Complaining puts God to the test, and there is a limit to the amount of complaining He will endure. When that limit is reached, only the faithful will obtain His promises. In choosing prayer targets, don't neglect to prayerfully and faithfully choose God's promises. Don't complain! Look beyond the circumstances to God's bountiful provision and redemptive purpose.

BATTLES RAGE ON THE EDGE OF VICTORY

In battle, problems are inevitable—they grow on the edge of triumph. Overcome the problems, and you gain the victory. Run from the problems, and you become a victim. Complaining and discontent on the verge of victory turn soldiers into casualties and free men into slaves. The battle rages most fiercely on the edge of victory. Therefore, do not run from the battle, run to it! Run toward your problems—they are where your victory will be gained!

Caleb saw differently than did the other Hebrew spies: He saw a great victory. He knew that once Israel defeated the giants, all their neighbors would fear them. When Joshua saw Jericho, he saw great victory. He knew that when Israel defeated Jericho, all their neighbors would fear them.

In David's time, when the Israelites saw Goliath, they saw a great defeat. But when David saw Goliath, he saw a great victory. He refused to rehearse his fears and instead proclaimed his triumph.

Instead of rehearsing our fears, we must declare our faith. Whiners never win, and winners never whine. Whining is vocalized unbelief, and unbelief is sin. Instead of being slaves to the sin of unbelief, which leads to death, we must choose to be slaves of faith and obedience, which leads us to righteousness and life.

Don't focus on the battle when choosing prayer targets. With eyes of faith, look at things not seen, and focus on the victory beyond the battle. Focus your faith in the future that God has prepared for you!

APPLICATION

KEY POINTS

(1) Conflict offers both combatants only two choices: yield or conquer.

(2) By default we have yielded to whatever remains unconquered.

(3) Complaining is nothing more than yielding to and confessing our fear of defeat.

(4) Complaining breeds discontent, and discontent is the seedbed of rebellion.

(5) Complaining puts God to the test, and there is a limit to the amount of complaining He will endure.

(6) Complaining and discontent turn soldiers into casualties and free men into slaves.

(7) Do not run from the edge of victory, where the battle rages most fiercely; run toward it!

(8) Complaining is vocalized unbelief, and unbelief is sin.

(9) When choosing prayer targets, focus on the victory beyond the battle.

(10) Focus your faith on the future, redemptive goal God has prepared for you!

SPIRITUAL RECONNAISSANCE

(1) What are the spiritual battles our community seems most afraid to face?

(2) What are our community's most common complaints?

(3) Which group or groups in our community seem most discontent, and what complaints (legitimate or not) have fostered that discontent?

(4) What groups in the community are exacerbating the complaints of others to foment rebellion and discontent in order to gain political support for their limited political agendas?

(5) In what ways are the community's complaints putting God to the

test and closing the heavens to our prayers and to His blessings?

(6) What social problems stand in the way of our community's growth and prosperity?

(7) How can we, as a Christian community, turn around each problem to see it from a "victory perspective," as an opportunity for kingdom advancement?

PERSONALIZE IT

(1) What are the spiritual battles I seem most afraid to face?

(2) What are my most common complaints?

(3) In what areas do I seem most discontented, and what complaints (legitimate or not) have fostered that discontent?

(4) What situations and/or individuals may be exacerbating my complaints to foment rebellion and discontent in my heart?

(5) In what ways are my complaints putting God to the test and closing the heavens to my prayers and to His blessings?

(6) What personal problems stand in the way of my spiritual growth and prosperity?

(7) How can I as a Christian turn around each problem to see it from a "victory perspective," as an opportunity for kingdom advancement in my life?

NEW THINKING

THE THINKING THAT CAUSED TODAY'S
PROBLEMS IS INSUFFICIENT TO SOLVE THEM.

T he thinking that caused today's problems is insufficient to solve them," said Albert Einstein. This wasn't his fatalistic proclamation of the world's end; it was his appeal for "new thinking." It's been said that repeatedly repeating the same action and expecting different results is insanity. Yet this is exactly what we do when we base today's and tomorrow's actions on yesterday's thinking. We can't solve problems with actions based on the thinking that produced them. If yesterday's thinking could solve today's problems, our problems would have been solved yesterday. To solve today's problems we must formulate new strategies based on today's new thinking.

INSPIRATION, EXPERIENCE,
AND OBSERVATION

New thinking requires a balanced blend of *inspiration*, *experience*, and *observation*.

▶ *Inspiration* comes from God and is based, in part, on our observations. By adequately analyzing our present situation, we become more aware of what resources are available and how they are related. By God's inspiration we arrange those resources to solve our problems. Inspiration shows us what new thing is possible.

▶ By our *experience* we confirm whether or not our plan will produce a plausible solution. We can't calculate the exact results of our new thinking by our experience, but we can know what's been possible or impossible in the past and speculate in general on future results. Experience shows us that our inspiration is reasonable.

▶ *Observation* shows us *how* an inspiration is possible, and experience shows us *why* it's possible.

Life sometimes presents us with a choice where there seems to be no good options—we feel forced to choose the lesser of two evils. At those times we need new thinking. In Russia, one young woman who wanted very much to be married and have children was diagnosed with uterine cancer. Doctors told her she had only two choices: eliminate her womb and her ability to bear children, or do nothing and die of cancer.

This is typical of the choices Satan gives people. However, in prayer, we receive inspiration to view our dilemma from a different perspective. God can and often does heal cancer when we believe and pray. But that requires new thinking! Our Russian friend chose to trust the Lord and is still alive today.

GOD-INSPIRED THINKING

As Moses faced the Red Sea, he apparently had three options: He could jump in and drown, challenge the Egyptian army and die in battle, or turn back, surrender, and return to slavery. To the natural mind none of these seems particularly encouraging or inspiring. But Moses wasn't viewing the circumstances with his natural mind. Who'd have guessed he would use a stick to part the Sea and that the Israelites would cross it without getting wet?

As David faced Goliath, his choices seemed depressing: He could face the giant and die in battle, leaving Israel under Philistine rule, or he could refuse to face Goliath and leave Israel's army demoralized. Who'd have guessed a mere boy could defeat Goliath with neither armor nor sword? Such actions are the result of new, God-inspired thinking!

REARRANGE YOUR RESOURCES

When we face desperate situations, what effect do our prayers really have? Prayer does not necessarily change our circumstances or the resources available to us to resolve the problem. What prayer does is change our understanding of the situation. The available resources are exactly the same as before we prayed; what changes is our knowledge of how to arrange and utilize them. As we observe each situation and pray to God, He inspires us to rearrange our resources to resolve our problems. He inspired Moses to lift the rod and part the sea. He inspired David to gather five smooth stones and take aim. And He inspires us to get the right tools into the right hands at the right time.

New thinking is required to discern and obtain the right tools and place them into the right hands. New thinking is required to get those hands working together in the ideal place at the ideal moment. If the right tools were already in the right hands at the right time, we wouldn't be faced with such hindrances to the preaching of the gospel.

The issue is this: Satan constantly rearranges his resources to maximize his effectiveness and to keep us off balance. Too often we apply old thinking and old methods to new problems and wonder why we're so ineffective. Why do we continue to expect new and effective results from antiquated ideas? We must constantly re-arrange our resources to counter the enemy's new strategies, all of which requires new thinking. God invites us to this: "If any of you lack wisdom, let him ask of God, that giveth to all men liberally, and upbraideth not; and it shall be given him" (James 1:5 KJV).

In new and desperate situations we must pray for new thinking. It's not easy to think as we've never thought before. We don't quickly recognize innovative solutions because we've yet to see them. We need God's inspiration!

Therefore, pray that you will receive His perspective on your situation. Pray also that He will inspire your leaders to see each problem from His perspective and that they will follow His plan to solve it. Pray for new thinking!

KEY POINTS

(1) Repeatedly repeating the same action and expecting different results each time is a form of insanity.

(2) We cannot expect to solve problems with actions based on the thinking that caused them.

(3) New thinking requires a balanced blend of God's inspiration and our observation and experience.

(4) It is a typical strategy of the devil to try to convince us that our choices are limited to those he offers.

(5) As we face desperate situations, God inspires us to rearrange our resources to resolve our problems.

(6) Satan constantly rearranges his resources to maximize his effectiveness and to keep us off balance.

(7) We must constantly rearrange our resources to counter the devil's new strategies.

(8) It's not easy to think like we've never thought before.

(9) We do not quickly recognize innovative solutions because we've never before seen them.

(10) *Pray for new thinking based on God's inspiration.*

SPIRITUAL RECONNAISSANCE

(1) What community problems seem consistently and stubbornly beyond resolution?

(2) Who are our community's key inspirational and experienced observers?

(3) Which problems in our community seem to offer only negative solutions?

(4) What are the intercessors, prophets, and apostles saying about these problems?

(5) How can the existing resources be rearranged to solve each problem?

(6) What are the right tools and who are the right people to bring about change in our community?

PERSONALIZE IT

(1) What personal problems seem consistently and stubbornly beyond resolution?

(2) Who are the key inspirational and experienced observers in my life?

(3) Which problems seem to offer only negative solutions?

(4) What are the Bible, my leaders, and my praying friends saying about these problems?

(5) How can the existing resources be rearranged to solve each problem?

(6) What are the right tools and who are the right people to bring about change in my life?

HISTORICAL CONTEXT

HISTORY IS THE ONE IMMOVABLE MOUNTAIN WITH WHICH THE MIND OF EVERY MAN MUST CONTEND.

It's been said that history is the one immovable mountain with which the mind of man must contend. Between that mountain and the destiny of mankind lies the broad wall of one's worldview. To some it is a wall of protection that shuts out a threatening world. To others it is a wall of oppression that restrains them from realizing freedom. Regardless of how one sees it, every person or group is poised on this wall between their historical context and their anticipated future. How one contends with this wall largely determines how pivotal or how marginal he will be to his generation.

WORLDVIEW FRONTIERS

One's present worldview is the frontier between past disappointments and future glories, or past glories and future disappointments. In any spiritual advance, the projected future will remain meaningless to those who have not shaped it according to the character of their historical context. That is to say, they'll reject any advance that ignores their historical context. The present worldview is a transitional wall that must take into account both past fears and past glories. These direct a person, in the relentless stream of time, toward an inevitable future. The future is inevitable; we can't stop it, but we can change it. The question is, "How will we face it?" Are we backing into the future?

Everyone stands on this frontier, the frontier of the present—we're not all looking the same way, but we're all looking one way or the other. Some look forward with hopeful expectancy of a better life. Others look back with mournful remorse to lost comforts, long past but not forgotten. In praying for a people of a particular historical context, the objective is to orient them toward the future without depriving them of their past securities. Sometimes this is possible, sometimes it's not. If it's not, any security relinquished must be replaced with a more reliable one.

THE CHARACTER OF THE PROVIDER

For the Israelites, the replacement for the past securities of Egypt (leeks, onions, cucumbers) was not manna, quail, or water. The replacement was the character of God. Provision is a reflection of the Provider. The main issue Israel faced in the desert was not lack of provision—they lacked knowledge of the Provider's character. Despite the hardships of four centuries of Egyptian bondage, they learned to trust in Pharaoh, whom they could see, over God, whom they could not see. God had proved to them Pharaoh's frailty and still they doubted Him. They wavered on the wall of their worldview between doubt and full faith. This restrained them from the freedom of their future, and that's what needed to change in the desert of their hearts and minds.

Reshaping people's worldview is more than defeating their past gods. It also requires building their trust in the Provider to where they rely on Him exclusively. When your allegiance is exclusive, your vision is clear. *Reshaping a worldview is an issue of allegiance.* Only when old allegiances have fully eroded away will people fully embrace the future benefits of a new one. As Scripture teaches, you don't put new wine into old wineskins. But how is trust in a new allegiance formed?

People's trust in a new allegiance is built by healing their wounds, redeeming their losses, and conquering their fears. These are the residue of history that establish our mindset and shape our decisions. Every battle is waged to alleviate, heal, or reconcile one of these. Wars are fought to alleviate fears, to heal the raging wounds of pride, and to reconcile losses. New allegiance requires a careful consideration of these historical issues.

HEAL WOUNDS

When oppression is evident in a society's history, it leaves unseen wounds on the hearts of its citizens. Though these wounds may not be apparent to outsiders, they are painfully and profoundly felt by insiders. If you strike an old wound, you'll discover its depth. It is for these wounds that the intercessor must gently and compassionately probe, because locked up in the scars of the past are the keys to the future. When we bring healing to the deepest wounds of a people's past, they begin to trust us. When they begin to trust us, we can begin to candidly direct them toward placing their trust in God. Though we may fail them, He never will.

ALLEVIATE SUFFERING

When deprivation is a society's historical hallmark, it colors the people's attitudes. Their worldview is polluted with want, and their fickle allegiance is held hostage to pressing need—they'll align themselves with whoever alleviates it. Though they don't know it, they withdraw from the most nourishing and reliable sources, at the whim of their wants, and then accuse the source from which they've withdrawn of being unreliable. They cannot know patience because they've trained themselves to believe that desire and deprivation are cut from the same fabric. If they have a desire, they feel it must be because they've been deprived. To them, desire is a reflection of loss.

This "deprivation syndrome" is perhaps the most complex web from which intercessors may strive to extract a people. Compassionate longevity is the key to their freedom. The "quick fix" of well-meaning donors has often only served to cement their conviction that they truly are deprived and consistently do suffer loss. Relationship, not provision, is the key to the unveiling of their eyes. But provision may be the spark you need to ignite long-term relationship.

CONQUER FEARS

When people are fearful, their fear is evidence of abandonment. At some point in their past, at what seemed to be their gravest hour of need, they felt abandoned. These unalleviated fears regenerate themselves most often, though not exclusively, through religious practices. Rituals express both fears and hopes for the future. Through rituals, people seek an alliance that will alleviate their fears and secure their future.

But fears cannot be placated; they must be conquered. The fears are inside, and you can only conquer the fears you're willing to confront. For instance, where abandonment has produced fear, avoidance of relationships is not the answer. Ritual is a placebo for relationships deemed too risky. Fears are not conquered through mental gymnastics; fears are conquered through covenant relationships.

When I (Eddie) was on staff at a large Texas church several years ago, a young woman was sent to me for counseling. She was about seventeen, the age (at the time) of my youngest son. Her problem?

She was incredibly fearful of men. Her mother, now single, had been through a couple of rough marriages. I don't remember all the details of her story, but I do remember how very fearful she was and how reluctant she was even to talk with me. She could barely look me in the eyes. I'll never forget an assignment I gave her one Saturday.

"Tomorrow, when you come to church, I want you to look me up and give me a hug."

She turned up her nose and shivered with disgust at the thought. She couldn't imagine being that close to a man—any man. When we stood to leave, I reached for her and she turned to stone. I extended one arm around her and patted her on the shoulder, like a father encouraging his daughter. It was like hugging a porcupine. I smiled and said, "There, that wasn't all that bad. I'll see you tomorrow."

The next morning, when I first caught a peripheral glimpse of her, I noticed that she saw me and hid behind a potted plant. I gradually made my way over and said, "Tough?" She nodded. I said, "I'll take the initiative." With that I patted her lightly on the shoulder and she relaxed.

Each week we kept to the assignment. And I watched as the fears of her past faded away. The day came when she'd see me, run over, and give me a hug without any fearful thought whatsoever. I had become like a good dad to her.

———

Two college years later I was told she had a boyfriend (her first). He visited our church a couple of times when he was in town. Then I learned they were engaged. Their wedding day came. Not so long thereafter I was delighted to see her, her loving husband, and her beautiful baby boy in our services. She told me they were in full-time Christian ministry. Her bravery to conquer her fears had opened up a whole new and blessed life for her.

"Heal the wounds, alleviate the suffering, and conquer the fears."
This dictum must be within the intercessory focus of any strategic advance. Left neglected, any perceived progress may only be superficial or temporary. Wounds, losses, and fears are rooted in the past and often only reveal themselves through time and covenant relationships. They are principal issues in the matrix of a historical context, and they are central both to understanding people's worldview and to their freedom in Christ.

A person is often marginalized by his perspective of the past. His view of history can motivate him either to overcome or to succumb to the challenges he faces. If his wounds are left unhealed, his losses unreconciled, and his fears unconquered, he'll respond negatively, either passively or aggressively, to the context of his past. If he responds negatively with aggression, he may become pivotal to his generation but will likely be remembered as a tyrant, not a benefactor.

When their wounds are healed, losses reconciled, and fears conquered, individuals, communities, and nations are able to respond positively to their historical context. *To move a person or a people, in a positive way, from a marginal role to a pivotal role, you must adequately address the issues of historical context.* Failure to do so can seriously hamper your efforts to introduce them to the ultimate Healer, Reconciler, and Conqueror.

APPLICATION

KEY POINTS

(1) Every person and every people is poised on the wall of their worldview between their historical context and their anticipated future.

(2) A person's generational influence is marginalized by his perspective of the past.

(3) The future is inevitable; there is nothing you can do to stop it, but you can change it.

(4) Reshaping a people's worldview is more an issue of building exclusive trust in the Provider than of defeating past gods.

(5) When your allegiance is exclusive, your vision is clear.

(6) Reshaping worldview is an issue of allegiance.

(7) New allegiances are built by healing wounds, redeeming losses, and conquering fears—these are the residue history has left in our minds.

    (a) *Heal wounds:* locked up in scars of the past are keys to the future.

    (b) *Alleviate suffering:* worldview is polluted with want, and allegiance is a victim of need.

    (c) *Conquer fears:* fear is evidence of feeling abandoned at one's gravest hour of need.

SPIRITUAL RECONNAISSANCE

(1) On the frontier of our community's dominant worldview, does it tend more to face the past or the future? Is the cup half empty or half full?

(2) On what or whom does our community tend to rely in place of God?

(3) What is our community's corporate wound most in need of healing?

(4) What is the greatest loss or source of suffering from our community's past?

(5) What is the greatest fear our community presently faces, and what is its historical context?

PERSONALIZE IT

(1) On the frontier of my worldview, do I tend more to face the past or the future? Is the cup half empty or half full?

(2) On what or whom do I tend to rely in place of God?

(3) What is the wound of my heart most in need of healing?

(4) What is the greatest loss or source of suffering from my past?

(5) What is the greatest fear I presently face, and what is its historical context?

PART 4

PROACTIVE
PRAYER

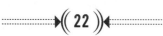
PRAYING THE PROMISES OF GOD

THE WORD, THE LOGOS, IS FULL
OF GOD-BREATHED PROMISES THAT
HE MUST FULFILL.

G od's Word, the *Logos* (here indicating the expression of His nature, will, and character made known as Scripture), is full of promises that He *must* fulfill. Is that a radical statement? Think of the alternative! What if God wasn't obliged to fulfill His Word? If God, for a moment, neglected to keep His Word, the fabric of the universe would unravel. To make a promise and not keep it is inconsistent with the character of the One who gave His own Son to die for our sins. He gave us His best—what cause would He have to withhold from us anything less?

God's Word *never* returns empty-handed. It *always* accomplishes the purpose for which it was spoken. But the Word is activated in our lives by our faith.

There is life-giving power in God's Word (Hebrews 4:12). Every word in the Bible is pregnant with life. This is what we cannot overlook: its potential is released by our obedience, faith, and prayer.

Without a word from God our faith is only presumption. Once we've received the seed of His Word for a given situation, that seed must be carefully *planted in the soil of our faith, watered with our prayers, and placed in the light of our worship* before it can produce a harvest.

Without the Word of God we have nothing and can do nothing for Him. Without faith, the seed of His Word has no mineral nutrient to nourish it. Without prayer, God's Word for our lives will shrivel and die; prayer makes the nutrients of faith available to the seed and root of the Word. Without our worship there is no spiritual photosynthesis (the process by which plants are nourished). Worship united with prayer provides God's Word the energy it needs to grow.

FAITH AND OBEDIENCE

God fashioned the universe by His Word. His prophets foretold events centuries into the future by His Word. He redeems us from our sin and adopts us as His sons by His living Word.

There is much potential in God's Word that has yet to be tapped in prayer. When we fail to pray according to His Word, we ignore His provision for our safety, comfort, empowerment, and well-being. But prayer is only half of the equation for empowerment. Through prayer God's will is *revealed;* by obedience God's will is *fulfilled.*

When we neglect to obey God's revealed Word, we leave our sword sheathed. No conqueror overcomes his enemy without first unsheathing his sword. God has given us many magnificent tools in His Word, but which we'll use is our choice. Tools are worthless until utilized. Knowledge is worthless until applied.

By faith, we obey God's Word. Where there's no obedience, there's no faith. For the Christian, where there's no faith there's also no victory: "Whatever is born of God overcomes the world; and this is the victory that has overcome the world—our faith" (1 John 5:4).

Years ago I (Eddie) said to an elderly pastor, "If God said it, I believe it, and that settles it."

He replied, "Son, if God said it, that settles it whether you believe it or not."

When we look at God's Word, the question isn't "Is anything there?" The question is "Will we believe it when we see it?" The Hebrews 11 heroes of faith are those who believed and acted on God's revealed Word. Our faith doesn't make it real—it's real whether or not we believe it.

STAND ON THE PROMISES

As we engage the devil in spiritual battle over regions and communities, we mustn't overlook God's abundant promises made known to us through His Word. He's granted us an inheritance as His sons, but until we learn to read His Word diligently, we'll remain ignorant of it. Until we learn to believe and obey His Word, it will remain powerless in our lives. We need to learn to pray the promises of God in faith.

But more than this, we must learn to stand on those promises. When crying out to Him for greater faith . . .

▶ Do we allow Him to place us in circumstances where greater faith is required?

▶ Do we pray for faith to heal the sick and then refuse to pray for the sick?

▶ Do we pray for faith to raise the dead and then refuse to lay hands on and pray for the dead? (The Western Christian sees far less of this than other nations. It's commonplace in many cultures today.)

After all, we'll not experience a miracle until we need one.

APPLICATION

KEY POINTS

(1) To make a promise and not keep it is inconsistent with the character of the One who gave His own Son to die for our sins.

(2) God's Word is activated in our lives by our faith in it.

(3) Faith without a word from God is only presumption.

(4) Without the Word of God we have nothing and can do nothing for Him.

(5) Without faith, the seed of God's Word has no soil to nourish it.

(6) When we neglect to pray according to God's Word we ignore the provision He's made for our safety, comfort, empowerment, and well-being.

(7) Through prayer God's will is revealed, but by obedience His will is performed.

(8) The heroes of our faith are those who believed and acted on God's revealed Word.

(9) When crying out to God for greater faith, do we allow Him to place us in circumstances where greater faith is required?

SPIRITUAL RECONNAISSANCE

(1) What God-breathed promises do our leaders, intercessors, and prophets seem most consistently to apply to our community's most pressing issues?

(2) How is God expecting our Christian community to act on these promises?

(3) As a Christian community, are we willing to allow God to place us publicly in positions and circumstances where greater faith is required of us?

PERSONALIZE IT

(1) What God-breathed promises are my leaders, my praying friends, and the Holy Spirit most consistently applying to my most pressing issues?

(2) How is God expecting me to act on these promises?

(3) As a Christian, am I willing to allow God to place me publicly in positions and circumstances where greater faith is required of me?

PRAYING THE PROPHECIES OF GOD

THROUGHOUT SCRIPTURE, IT IS GOD'S RHEMA
WORD THAT REVEALS THE PROPHETIC
SIGNIFICANCE OF PEOPLE, PLACES, AND
THE TIMES IN WHICH THEY LIVE.

In May 1989, in Caracas, Venezuela, one year after becoming a missionary, I (Michael) was walking out of Las Acasias Church with my future wife when a young woman stopped us. She said she'd had a prophetic dream in which God had told her to pray for us because He wanted to use us as missionaries in Russia. She'd been looking for us for three weeks; the dream had been so vivid that she could still sing back to us the songs we'd been singing in it.

Honestly, we wondered if she was a flake. Didn't she know the Iron Curtain was closed? For several years we filed the prophecy away and thought nothing further of it while we continued to minister in Venezuela.

Three years later in America, while listening to a sermon by Dr. Michael Brown, we fell under conviction that our hearts were growing cold. His message that day had been, "If you are not growing closer to God, then you are falling away." We'd returned from the field for a year of training and preparation. Frankly, we returned because we were burned out. We still wanted to be missionaries but didn't want to get burned out again. I'd started seminary training with Dr. Brown and others, but gradually we felt our passion for the Lord and our passion for souls slipping away. That was the state we were in when the Holy Spirit arrested us that morning.

Under the Spirit's conviction, first my wife and then I made our way to the front to weep and pray in the Lord's presence. Under that anointing, though I intended to whisper it, I began to cry out, as Isaiah did, "Here am I. Send me." With tears streaming down my face, and with my wife in the same condition, I'm sure many thought we were repenting of some terrible secret sin. But God was speaking to us from His presence. As we lay on the floor, He told each of us separately that we were to go to Russia.

After the service, we compared notes and decided this was a serious enough matter to merit further prayer. We prayed a couple hours more and then kept an appointment to meet with our closest friends. When we told them what we'd heard, the wife, known for her accurate prophetic dreams, began to jump up and down. She shared that she'd recently had a vivid dream of us ministering in Russia. Believe it or not, we *still* didn't know what to do next.

After further prayer over a period of months, we decided it would be best for me to go to Minister's Training Institute for further mission preparation. With the blessing of my leaders at Beth Messiah Congregation in Gaithersburg, Maryland, I was released for another year of Bible Institute in Louisiana, specifically for missionary training, before returning to the field.

While there, we met again with the GSMA Missions Director Dick Bashta (whom we'd met in 1989) and decided to attend his church. In December 1992, with no foreknowledge of the previous words we'd received from the Lord, Dick asked us to consider going to Russia. We said we would pray about it, and we did.

Finally one Sunday, after feeling we'd exhausted our excuses for not going, and after feeling the Spirit's leading to make a decision that morning, I said, "Aimee, I think we're supposed to tell Dick today that we're willing to go to Russia."

She replied, "I just need one more undeniable word from God."

At precisely that moment, a worship-team member jumped from his position on the stage and ran to us. "I can't hold back any longer," he said. "I've got to pray for you." With no foreknowledge of the decision we were pondering, he proceeded to pray and prophesy about our future on the Russian mission field. As you can imagine, that morning we accepted God's invitation to Russia.

RHEMA AND THE PROPHETIC PROCESS

Prophetic words from God can take many forms. The most important form is His written Word (*Logos*). Nevertheless, it is by the revealed Word (*rhema*) that we understand how the written Word applies to our time. *Rhema* is the life-changing inspiration of the Holy Spirit. *Rhema* turns our knowledge of Scripture into a saving knowledge.

It was *rhema* that allowed Daniel to understand the times prophesied by Jeremiah (see Daniel 9:2). It was by *rhema* that John the Baptist proclaimed, "I am the voice of one calling in the desert, 'Make straight the way for the Lord'" (John 1:23 NIV). Throughout Scripture, it is God's *rhema* Word that reveals the prophetic significance of people, places, and the times in which they live.

Certain prophecies in the Word, such as the birth, life, death, and resurrection of Jesus, have been definitively fulfilled. Others are in the process of fulfillment (such as the restoration of national Israel).

There are also prophecies that have been fulfilled, in part as a foreshadowing of something yet to come. For example, some consider the exodus account to be a prophetic picture of the total redemption of mankind—accomplished in part by Jesus' death as the Passover Lamb and to be accomplished in full by the Joshua who will lead God's people into their final inheritance. (*Jesus* and *Joshua* derive from the same name, meaning "Savior.")

Finally, there are those "words" that, as far as we know, are not yet being fulfilled (e.g., the great tribulation).

Praying accurately for God's prophecies to be fulfilled requires a working knowledge of His Word. Many false prophets could have been saved from the error of their ways if they'd only better known the Word. Every believer should know and understand the basic principles of biblical interpretation. Our cities are rife with sometimes well-intentioned cults whose doctrines are unbiblical and, in some cases, anti-biblical. Yet each of these considers itself to be Christian, and some claim they are the only *true* Christians.

Praying accurately for fulfillment of God's prophecies also requires a working knowledge of His character. *God will never act contrary to His character.* But if you don't know Him, you won't know His character, and you may be tempted to pray for things inconsistent with His character and will.

Finally, praying accurately for God's prophecies to be fulfilled requires some Holy Spirit discernment as to which of four stages a specific prophetic word falls into.

(1) Is it fulfilled?

(2) Is it being fulfilled?

(3) Is it fulfilled in part as a foreshadowing of something yet to come?

(4) Is it not yet being fulfilled?

FULFILLED AND BEING FULFILLED

If a prophetic word has been *fulfilled*, there's no need to pray for it further. If a prophetic word is *being fulfilled*, pray for the accomplishment of that word in a way that will be consistent with the rest of God's Word, character, and revealed will.

Praying for a word that is being fulfilled requires a different strategy than praying for a word that is not yet being fulfilled. If a word is *being fulfilled*, we need a sense of the timing, the individuals involved, their circumstances, and the history of the situation that gave rise to its eminent fulfillment.

FULFILLED IN PART

If a prophetic word is *fulfilled in part* as a foreshadowing of something yet to come, then we should pray that our generation will be awakened to the urgency of the hour and to the role we must play to bring about its fulfillment. In those cases, we have to pray rather generally. We cannot pray specifically until the Spirit reveals specific details to us, or until time progresses and the word is *being fulfilled*.

NOT YET FULFILLED

Praying for a word that is *the foreshadowing of a coming event* and a word that is *not yet being fulfilled* require attention to a whole different set of details. Here we don't usually know the timing (though we may sense or suspect it). We don't typically know the individuals involved or the circumstances surrounding them. And, we don't have the benefit of hindsight. Discernment of this sort is the exclusive competence of the Holy Spirit. We can only arrive at this level of discernment through the *rhema* Word of God as we fellowship with the Spirit in prayer.

PROPHETIC SEED

Paul exhorts Timothy,

> This command I entrust to you, Timothy, my son, in accordance with the prophecies previously made concerning you, that by them you [may] fight the good fight, keeping faith and a good conscience. (1 Timothy 1:18–19)

Apparently we're able to fight a good fight with the prophetic words made concerning us; this sounds like a strategic use of prophecy. Later Paul says, "Do not neglect the spiritual gift within you, which was bestowed upon you through prophetic utterance" (4:14). There's a level of personal prophecy we must lay hold of with faithful prayer. We must not neglect it. Unless we plant that prophetic word in the soil of faith, water it with prayer, and place it in the light of our worship unto God, that prophetic seed will produce nothing in our lives. In contrast, properly planted, watered, and enriched through worship, that word can result in the salvation of others.

Let's pray that we will be more diligent to study the Scriptures and more accurately discern the times, the Word, and the will of God. Let's pray for an ever-increasing sensitivity to the Holy Spirit. And let's pray that God's prophetic *rhema* Word, once revealed, would come alive in our hearts and minds so we will speak to our generation and not remain silent.

KEY POINTS

(1) Praying accurately for God's prophecies to be fulfilled requires a working knowledge of His Word and character.

(2) Praying accurately for God's prophecies to be fulfilled requires Holy Spirit discernment as to which of four stages a specific prophetic word falls into.

    (a) Is it *fulfilled*?

    (b) Is it *being fulfilled*?

    (c) Is it *fulfilled in part* as a foreshadowing of something yet to come?

    (d) Is it *not yet being fulfilled*?

(3) If a prophetic word is fulfilled, there's no need to pray for it further.

(4) If a prophetic word is being fulfilled, we pray for its accomplishment in a way that's consistent with all of God's Word, character, and will; also, in a way that would awaken the hearts of our generation to the urgency of the hour and to the concrete role we must play to bring it about.

(5) Praying for a word that is the foreshadowing of a coming event and for a word that is not yet being fulfilled require discernment through God's *rhema* Word as we fellowship with the Holy Spirit in prayer.

(6) Strategic use of prophecy enables us to fight a good fight with the prophetic words made concerning us.

SPIRITUAL RECONNAISSANCE

(1) What prophetic words are the leaders and recognized prophets and intercessors in our region consistently declaring over our community's most pressing issues?

(2) Are these prophetic words consistent with God's character?

(3) At what stage in the prophetic process is each of these words?

Fulfilled? Being fulfilled? Partially fulfilled as a foreshadowing of something yet to come? Not yet being fulfilled?

(4) As a Christian community, what faith-filled prophetic response to these words does God expect from us?

PERSONALIZE IT

(1) What prophetic words are my leaders and praying friends declaring over the most pressing issues of my life?

(2) Are these prophetic words consistent with God's character?

(3) At what stage in the prophetic process is each of these words? Fulfilled? Being fulfilled? Partially fulfilled as a foreshadowing of something yet to come? Not yet being fulfilled?

(4) What faith-filled prophetic response to these words does God expect from me?

PRAYING FOR THE GIFTS OF GOD

THE GIFTS OF GOD TO MEN HAVE STRATEGIC
DESIGN AND PURPOSE.

God is a God of purpose, intentional in all He does, and He gives gifts to accomplish His intended purposes. In the same way He endows individuals with spiritual gifts by the Holy Spirit, so too He endows congregations, communities, and nations with distinctive spiritual gifts according to the Spirit's will.

God endows individuals, communities, and nations with gifts designed to help lead the nations to Christ. The church's primary purpose is to win souls and make disciples; God designs and strategically distributes spiritual gifts for the church with this overall purpose in mind. It's time for the church to become as strategic about the placement and use of the Spirit's gifts as the military is about the placement and use of its weaponry.

Here are a few observations about the spiritual gifts granted to individuals that might give us a clearer picture of how to pray for the distribution of gifts in the body of Christ.

UNEQUAL DISTRIBUTION

Observation One: Certain gifts are more prevalent than others. Each gift does *not* have equal distribution throughout Christ's body: the Holy Spirit "works all these things, distributing to each one individually just as He wills" (1 Corinthians 12:11). Only the Spirit has the wisdom and foresight to discern what gift to accent, where, and at what time. Neither each person nor every community needs the same emphasis on a particular gift at the same time because each has its own assignment.

Generally, the whole body needs all the gifts all the time. But the body needs only two eyes while it needs ten fingers. All members of the body serve the body, but the service of each varies according to ability and purpose.

PLACEMENT

Observation Two: The ability of each member is determined, in part, by its placement in the body. A misplaced body part is useless. A member cannot do what it's called to do when improperly positioned. Certain parts belong alongside certain other parts—efficient work can occur in no other way. Applying this principle spiritually, when we consider the Spirit's gifts, the placement of the gifts in the body of Christ is of great importance and should be prayed for accordingly.

GIFT ACCOUNTABILITY

In this respect, a major difference between the body of Christ and the human body is that the members of Christ's body are mobile, whereas the members of our human bodies, unlike some church members, tend to stay put. The gifts of the Spirit move around with people. Where people know how to humble themselves and cooperate with other parts, this can work to great advantage.

But where spiritual pride and ignorance of spiritual gifts prevail, results can be disastrous. There must be accountability for the effective use of the Spirit's gifts in the church. That accountability should be inherent in covenant relationships.

Covenant relationships take time to build. People who drift from one congregation to another never give their gifts opportunity to become rooted in a set of relationships that will enable their gifts to grow and operate most freely. Part of praying for God's gifts should include praying for gift accountability, which is the exclusive domain of covenant relationships.

There is no such thing as remote accountability. Accountability always proceeds along close relational lines. No relationship, no accountability; no accountability, no gift effectiveness.

In the same way that relationship with God governs the distribution of the Spirit's gifts, relationships should govern the delegation of spiritual responsibilities within the church. Though both "the apostle Paul" and "the apostle Peter" (or so they called themselves) came to my (Michael's) young congregation in Russia to preach, I did not let them come to the pulpit to share because I didn't know them. When they went away miffed and spouting curses, I knew I'd made the right decision.

I (Eddie) counseled with a pastor who saw his church of more than three hundred dissipate to a paltry few. He said it all began when "a prophetess" visited one day and in the midst of the service stood (in the audience) and began to prophesy over the congregation.

"Can I tell you what she said?" I asked.

Somewhat startled, he said, "You weren't there. You wouldn't know what she said."

"The enemy's not that creative, to be honest," I reminded him. "She likely said, 'My dear people, I love thee. This day I have sent unto thee my handmaiden. . . . '" (Why we're to accept that God would be so out of touch as to speak to twenty-first-century people in fifteenth-century English is beyond me.)

He gasped. "That's almost word for word what she said. And within two weeks she was conducting home meetings with our ladies, without my knowledge. And before long several of our leading families were dropping out to follow her. We had sixteen people in attendance last Sunday morning."

His mistake? Allowing just anyone to address his congregation; he didn't know her, much less know her well. There is perhaps no higher responsibility for a shepherd than to protect sheep from wolves in sheep's clothing. The elders are watchmen who must never desert the gates!

GIFTED BY RELATIONSHIP

Observation Three: Gifts are granted on the basis of relationship. This is true even in the natural world; why should it be any different in the spiritual realm? We give gifts to those we love and know and to those who have demonstrated sufficient maturity to use them wisely. I believe God does the same thing. If we truly love Him, He knows that He can trust us with His gifts.

If we are immature, even if we truly love Him, He will sometimes withhold certain gifts from us. If we do not love Him, we lack the key characteristic that qualifies us for giftedness: *Our love for God best positions us for maturity in the body of Christ.* And the evidence of our love for Him is that we will lay down our lives for each other (see 1 John 3:16).

As I (Eddie) often jokingly say, "I've been in the ministry more than four decades. I've met many Christians who would rather lay down my life for them than lay down their lives for me."

GIFTED BY DESIGN

Observation Four: God gives gifts according to His purpose. God's one great purpose for the universal body of Christ is the salvation of mankind. The gifts of the Spirit will pass away—there will be no place in heaven for their use. The only place for the use of the Spirit's gifts is in the midst of lost humanity.

God desires to redeem mankind and will use all available means to do it. To individuals, He gives spiritual gifts. To nations, He gives redemptive gifts. *All* the gifts are intended for the salvation of souls. The gifts are designed to fulfill a purpose, and we are gifted according to God's redemptive design.

Regarding spiritual gifts, an abundance of material is already available. (In particular, we recommend *Your Spiritual Gifts Can Help Your Church Grow* by C. Peter Wagner [Regal, 1994].) For the sake of prayer, let us here point out the twenty-five spiritual gifts Wagner lists in his "Wagner-Modified Gifts Questionnaire":

> Prophecy, Teaching, Knowledge, Discerning, Helps, Missionary, Hospitality, Leadership, Miracles, Tongues, Poverty, Intercession, Service, Pastor, Wisdom, Exhortation, Giving, Mercy, Evangelist, Faith, Administration, Healing, Interpretation, Celibacy, Exorcism

My (Eddie's) wife, Alice Smith, has a wonderful audio/video teaching, *Corporate Intercession*, that goes into great depth about how spiritual gifts work together in effective shared prayer (see at *www.PrayerBookstore.com*). It should come as no surprise that a person with the gift of mercy will pray differently, and probably have a different prayer assignment, than a person with the gift of prophecy.

Where any gift is absent or lacking in a congregation, there will be a ripple effect throughout the congregation and even the regional body of Christ. Not every church will have every gift active in equal degree, but all churches should have all the gifts active in at least some degree.

REDEMPTIVE GIFTS

Redemptive gifts are gifts granted to a group of people to help them point the way to Christ. Togliatti, Russia, is an excellent example of a city having a redemptive gift. This river city, originally named Stavropol ("place of the cross" in Old Russian), was established along the southern Volga River as a missionary outpost for the spread of the gospel. Under Stalin, Stavropol was buried under the rising waters of the new hydroelectric dam downstream of the city. The dam was built by prison labor, and many political prisoners (Christians among them) lost their lives during construction.

In the natural, one might think that Stavropol's redemptive purpose—to be a light to the region—was buried with the old city. But the redemptive gift remains with Togliatti, the city that grew up alongside the new dam. *The hydroelectric plant provides electricity for the entire region.* It's a source of light in the natural, and the area is still intended to be a source of light in the spiritual. Ultimately, the works of darkness cannot bury God's redemptive purposes.

An example of a national redemptive gift is Israel, endowed with the redemptive responsibility of being a blessing, a light, to the nations (see Genesis 12). Because of this, everyone who curses Israel will be cursed. We can say that the nation of Israel has been a greater source of blessing to the world's peoples than has been any other single nation on earth. Without fear of contradiction, we can also say that Israel has been a stumbling block to all who have cursed her. As a nation, more than any other, it points the way to God. That is its redemptive gift.

In conclusion, perhaps the most pressing prayer regarding spiritual gifts is prayer for the leaders of congregations, communities, and nations to discern the redemptive gifts with which they've been corporately endowed.

▶ Pray that God will accelerate and enlarge the revelation of their redemptive purpose and that their decisions would increasingly reflect that revelation.

▶ Pray that Christian leaders will understand the importance of all the Spirit's gifts both for their own congregations and for their communities.

▶ Pray that they will welcome and encourage the use of these gifts among their members.

KEY POINTS

(1) Individuals, congregations, communities, and nations can all be endowed by the Holy Spirit with distinct spiritual gifts.

(2) The Spirit's gifts are designed for use in the midst of lost humanity.

(3) We are all gifted according to God's redemptive design.

(4) Each gift does *not* have an equal distribution throughout Christ's body.

(5) Ability to function in your gifting depends on your placement in the body.

(6) The gifts of the Spirit move around with the people to whom they are given.

(7) Gift accountability is the exclusive domain of covenant relationships.

(8) Gifts are granted on the basis of relationship.

(9) Gifts are granted according to God's purposes.

SPIRITUAL RECONNAISSANCE

(1) What spiritual gifts seem to dominate or to be absent in our church?

(2) What seem to be the predominant spiritual gifts of other congregations in our region, and how does the gifting of our church seem to

fit into our region's overall gift-mix?

(3) How well does our church relate to surrounding churches in regard to transient members and accountability for the use of the Holy Spirit's gifts?

(4) Is our church, by virtue of its governing structure, doctrinal positions, or habitual pattern of worship, limiting our corporate intimacy with God and thereby the number, type, and intensity of spiritual gifts that can flow freely in our midst?

(5) As a church in the context of our community and region, what is our corporate redemptive purpose in God and in the universal body of Christ?

(6) Does our city, region, or country seem to have a redemptive gift? If so, what are the key indicators that most clearly identify it?

PERSONALIZE IT

(1) What spiritual gifts seem to dominate or to be absent in my life?

(2) What seem to be the predominant spiritual gifts of other family members, and how does my gifting seem to fit into my family's overall gift-mix?

(3) How well do I relate to my leaders and to other Christians in regard to covenant relationships and accountability for the use of the Spirit's gifts?

(4) Am I, by virtue of my daily schedule, doctrinal positions, or habitual pattern of worship, limiting my intimacy with God and thereby the number, type, and intensity of spiritual gifts that can flow freely through me?

(5) As a Christian in the context of my local church, what is my redemptive purpose in God and in the universal body of Christ?

(6) Does my family seem to have a redemptive gift? If so, what are the key indicators that most clearly identify it?

PRAYING FOR THE POWER OF GOD

THOUGH MEN CAN DENY GOD'S EXISTENCE, THEY CANNOT ESCAPE HIS POWER.

My message and my preaching were not in persuasive words of wisdom, but in demonstration of the Spirit and of power, that your faith should not rest on the wisdom of men, but on the power of God. (1 Corinthians 2:4–5)

From the creation account in Genesis, through the flood of Noah and the exodus of Moses, to the advent of Jesus' New Testament ministry and beyond, the power of God has been an uncomfortable intruder in the affairs of men. Though some deny His existence and power, they cannot escape His influence. God's power is proclaimed everywhere in every man's conscience and in all of creation. Though it can be denied, such denial is inexcusable.

GOD'S POWER PROCLAIMED

God proclaims His power through His Word and works. Jesus did not hide the fact of God's power but boldly proclaimed it to the Jews.

If I do not do the works of My Father, do not believe Me; but if I do them, though you do not believe Me, believe the works, that you may know and understand that the Father is in Me, and I in the Father. (John 10:37–38)

God's Word and works are endued with His power. Given God's nature, His Word and His works are inseparable from His power, and those who "believe in Him whom He has sent" (John 6:29) will do greater works than those Jesus performed! (John 14:10–12).

"HE GAVE THEM POWER"

Everything that exists is a demonstration of God's power. If it were interrupted for one millisecond, life in the physical universe would unravel. All creation, spiritual and material, is wrapped in and held together by God's power, and He desires that the faith of men rest on this power.

This is the power Jesus shared with His disciples when He *"gave them power and authority* over all the demons, *and to heal diseases,"* and sent them out *"to proclaim the kingdom of God, and to perform healing"* (Luke 9:1–2). He proclaimed the breadth of that power by saying, *"Behold, I have given you authority to tread upon serpents and scorpions, and over all the power of the enemy, and nothing shall injure you"* (10:19).

Jesus empowered them by the Holy Spirit to preach the gospel (Acts 1–2), which "is the power of God for salvation to everyone who believes" (Romans 1:16). He empowered His followers to be His ambassadors, that through us men might be reconciled to God (2 Corinthians 5:20). The disciples *"went out and preached everywhere, while the Lord worked with them, and confirmed the word by the signs that followed"* (Mark 16:20). God wants to demonstrate His power through His children. There are few greater joys a man can have than to see His son or daughter follow in his footsteps and carry on the family calling. Working within us is our Father's power—the power that raised Christ from the dead.

▸ *Authority* is the right to exercise God's power.

▸ *Anointing* is the power to exercise God's authority.

POWER ACCOUNTABILITY

Leave the power of God out of the Bible and you have nothing. God wants us to recognize His heart regarding His power. He gives it to us for the sake of His people and to fulfill His purposes. But too often we receive His power thinking we've earned the privilege to use it, and, therefore, we think we deserve the right to call it our own.

No. God's power does not belong to us. It belongs to Jesus and is only issued to us to carry out His will for mankind. All authority and power in heaven and on earth has been given to Jesus. If it all belongs to Him, then none of it belongs to anyone else (not you, not me, and certainly not the devil). Anyone who uses God's power according to his own will, and not according to the purpose of the One who authorized its use, is a usurper who will not escape punishment. God will hold us accountable for how we use His power and authority.

Pray that men will recognize the great power available to those who believe in the Son of God. Pray that those who are partakers of Christ's resurrection power would properly esteem that privilege and use God's power according to His will and authority.

)(APPLICATION)(

KEY POINTS

(1) God proclaims His power through His Word and works.
(2) God's Word and works are inseparable from His power.

(3) All life, spiritual and material, is wrapped and held together in God's power.

(4) Through Jesus and the work of the Spirit, God shares His power with man.

(5) God wants to demonstrate His power through His children.

(6) If you leave the power of God out of the Bible, you have nothing left.

(7) Too often, we receive God's power thinking we've *earned* the privilege to use it, and, therefore, we think we deserve the right to call it our own.

(8) The power of God belongs to man only in the person of Jesus and is delegated to us only to carry out His will for mankind.

(9) All authority and power in heaven and on earth has been given to Jesus, and none of it belongs to anyone else.

(10) God will hold you accountable for how you use His power and authority.

SPIRITUAL RECONNAISSANCE

(1) How is God's power evident to the community in the works of our local church?

(2) Does that power truly extend God's kingdom in our community, or is such growth imagined or restricted to the local body of believers?

(3) Does our community associate our local church with the miracles of God?

(4) Is our local church adequately aware of the power available to them in Christ?

(5) Do the members of our local church pray boldly for the needs of others (saved and pre-saved), thereby allowing God's power to flow through them?

PERSONALIZE IT

(1) How do my works make God's power evident to others?

(2) Does that power truly extend God's kingdom among my unsaved

family and friends, or is such growth imagined or restricted to my believing friends?

(3) Do others associate my life with the miracles of God?

(4) Am I adequately aware of God's power available to me in Christ Jesus?

(5) Do I pray boldly for the needs of others (saved and pre-saved), thereby allowing God's power to flow through me?

PRAYING FOR THE PRESENCE OF GOD

My Presence will go with you, and I
will give you rest. (Exodus 33:14 nkjv)

As I (Michael) entered the classroom to teach Hebrew, I was shocked by what I saw. It was 1994; Aimee and I had started a Bible school to train future ministers for our church. She'd been teaching that morning on the attributes of God, and as she taught, the students began to fall over in His presence. When I came in, God's palpable presence was still thick, and my eleven students didn't look much like students anymore.

However, dogged as I am in my German character, I decided to press on and teach Hebrew regardless. I knew it was important to guard God's presence but didn't yet know how to let the Holy Spirit preempt my program. Amazingly, I taught Hebrew, in English with a Russian translator, for one hour in the presence of the Lord, which remained uninterrupted through the duration.

Praise God that somehow I had avoided grieving the Spirit. When my class, the last one of the day, concluded, we could no longer continue with business as usual. The Spirit arrested us. All who were able decided to remain and worship in God's presence.

We worshiped for hours that seemed like minutes. When finally the time for our evening prayer meeting drew near, we quieted ourselves and waited for the doorbell to begin ringing. While more than forty people jammed into our little room, the presence of God remained. As Aimee led worship, almost from the first note people began to fall over. No one had discussed with anyone what happened earlier that day, and the people falling over were not Bible school students. God was still at work.

We continued in prayer, in worship, and in the reading of the Word until eleven. At that meeting, for the first time in my life, I saw people that looked truly "drunk" in the Holy Spirit. After that night, we (as a group) never again felt such an intense presence of the Lord. By His sovereign will God had invaded our lives for a moment, and we were forever changed. More than all our teaching, this single visitation cemented the resolve and commitment of our church leaders to pursue God.

One mid–1980s Sunday in Houston, our worship service began at 8:30 A.M. From the first moment we sensed an awe-inspiring divine presence. God often graced us with a momentary discernible visitation, but this was much greater than anything we'd ever experienced. As I (Eddie) led in worship it was clear that the preaching pastor wasn't going to be coming to the pulpit. His face was buried in the carpet as he profoundly and personally engaged with God.

Soon it was time for the Sunday school hour. But no one could move. We were all captivated by the Son of God.

As that hour should have ended, people began coming into the sanctuary for the eleven o'clock worship hour. But the building was packed; dozens were on their faces at the altar. Again, nobody had said one single word since we began at 8:30!

When we concluded at 2:30 P.M., eighteen adults had been born again. Lives were radically changed. For years to come that single service, where the Lord's presence was so real it could be felt, was the topic of conversation. And once you've experienced God's presence like this, you'll crave it for a lifetime. It is a foretaste of heaven.

There is one prayer target that, if reached, will not only radically change your future, it will also radically change your influence and relationship with others. In our personal search for prayer targets that will make our ministries more effective, one target remains elusive. We know what the target *is*, but honestly we've not yet consistently *reached* it. We're certain that when we do, we and those to whom we minister will be changed forever. So we continue to aim for that target, striving daily to reach it in prayer. What prayer target could possibly have such dramatic results?

To Dwell in the Presence of God

In Exodus 33:13, in the midst of interceding for his people's destiny, Moses makes some bold requests:

> *Now therefore, I pray, if I have found grace in Your sight, show me now Your way, that I may know You and that I may find grace in Your sight. And consider that this nation is Your people.* (NKJV)

From the context (v. 12), we see why Moses asked this. God had commanded him to *"bring up this people,"* but He hadn't let Moses know how to accomplish the task. Moses understood the goal but didn't know the way. He also knew he couldn't reach the goal in his own strength—he knew he needed help. And though God had said to him, *"I know you by name, and you have also found grace in My sight,"* He had not yet revealed who would help or how. So Moses said, *"You have not let me know whom You will send with me."*

What an audacious prayer! Who was this Moses who would make such a bold request of the Lord? According to verse 11, *"The Lord spoke to Moses face to face, as a man speaks to his friend."* Moses was God's friend. He was known by God, by name, and had found grace in His sight.

Moses' request reflected his knowledge of God's character. The Lord didn't rebuke him for being so bold; to the contrary, He responded, *"My Presence will go with you, and I will give you rest"* (v. 14). Then Moses knew that God himself would go with this people and replied,

> *If Your Presence does not go with us, do not bring us up from here. For how then will it be known that Your people and I have found grace in Your sight, except You go with us? So we shall be separate, Your people and I, from all the people who are upon the face of the earth.* (vv. 15–16)

GOD'S PRESENCE IS HIS WAY

We glean several principles from these passages. First, when Moses asked, *"Show me Your way"* (v. 13), God responded, *"My Presence will go with you"* (v. 14). God's presence is His way, and His way is His presence! Too often we seek to accomplish the work of the Spirit in the strength of the flesh. We attempt to fulfill His purposes without His presence. What we need most is to wait and seek God's presence, not anxiously moving ahead in our own strength and presumption. We don't wait for God's presence, but we still expect His grace. We don't understand what Moses *did* understand: that God's grace is experienced in His presence.

PRESENCE REVEALS GRACE

God's grace is *made known* by His presence. If His presence is not with us, His grace is not apparent to others; it is only in God's presence that His unmistakable grace becomes visible. The presence of God distinguishes and sets us apart from others—it "separates" the holy from the profane. God's people ought to be identified by His presence, and when we are, the peoples of the earth will know that He has sent us.

With this in mind, let us pray with renewed vigor for the presence of God. Pray that He will show you His way; that He will go with you. And do *not* try to accomplish His purposes without His power. Pray for His presence!

APPLICATION

KEY POINTS

(1) Our attitude toward God's presence ought to be the same as that of Moses: "If Your Presence does not go with us, do not lead us up from here."

(2) God's presence is His way, and His way is His presence!

(3) God's grace is in His presence, and it's in God's presence that we experience His grace.

(4) Only in God's presence does His unmistakable grace become apparent to others.

(5) The presence of God "separates" the holy from the profane.

(6) The people of God ought to be identifiable by the presence of God.

(7) By God's presence the peoples of the earth will know that God has sent us and that we have found grace in His sight.

(8) In God's presence is His grace to accomplish His will.

SPIRITUAL RECONNAISSANCE

(1) Does our congregation consistently experience and allow itself to be arrested by God's presence?

(2) Are our leaders and members aware of and consistently yielded to God's abiding presence in their daily lives?

(3) Does corporate knowledge of God's character allow our congregation to go boldly to the throne of grace to make audacious kingdom requests of Him?

(4) Does our congregation more consistently follow the cloud of God's presence or its own agenda?

(5) Do others recognize God's presence and grace in our congregation and in our corporate identity?

PERSONALIZE IT

(1) Do I consistently experience and allow myself to be arrested by God's presence?

(2) Am I aware of and consistently yielded to God's abiding presence in my daily life?

(3) Does my knowledge of God's character allow me to go boldly to the throne of grace to make audacious kingdom requests of Him?

(4) Do I more consistently follow the cloud of God's presence or my own agenda?

(5) Do others recognize God's presence and grace in me and in my family and home?

PRAYING FOR THE GLORY OF GOD

PLEASE, SHOW ME YOUR GLORY.
(EXODUS 33:18 NKJV)

O ne summer Sunday in 1985, God invaded my (Michael's) life in an unforgettable way. I'd been a believer for less than a year, but my heart burned with passion for God and for souls. As I stood that morning in church, worshiping with all my heart, it seemed as if heaven had split open and was about to dump all its treasures on me. God was pouring out His love directly into my heart. I felt as if I were looking into His face, as if my heart would burst. His love, His character, and His holiness were so pure and so intense.

As I drew nearer to Him in worship, His holy love seemed to draw nearer to me until it became unbearable. I could no longer gaze upon the purity of His love, nor could I continue to stand silently in the intensity of His loving presence. Thinking I would cry out and interrupt the service, I begged Him to stop revealing His love to me or I would die. At that moment, the pastor quieted the worship team and asked if anyone wanted to accept Jesus as Lord and Savior. Out of a gathering of nine hundred, only one woman raised her hand. She was seated directly behind me, and as she made her way to the stage to pray and repent, the Spirit whispered, "Such is My love for the worst of sinners." If that's His love for the worst of sinners, how much more intense could His love be?

"SHOW ME YOUR GLORY"

Beyond praying for God's presence, Moses prayed what must be the most audacious prayer in the entire Bible. In Exodus 33:18, he makes an incredible request: *"Please, show me Your glory"* (NKJV). This short prayer forever changed his life and his understanding of God. It changed the heart of the people toward God and toward Moses. To fully appreciate the profound depth of this remarkable prayer, we must remind ourselves who prayed it. The pat answer is that Moses prayed. But who was Moses? What had been imprinted on his character? What experience had formed his relationship with God? *Who was Moses?*

The Moses who prayed to see God's glory was a man who knew of his own miraculous rescue from the waters of the Nile. This was a man who had seen the world's glory in all its splendor. A prince among men, acquainted with abundance, with power, with respect, and with immeasurable wealth.

This was a son of Pharaoh, who escaped the hand of his anger by fleeing into the Midian desert. This was a man who stood before a burning bush, speaking with the God of Abraham, Isaac, and Jacob. This was the shepherd sent by the great "I AM" to rescue the people of Israel from slavery.

He'd witnessed the ten plagues and the defeat of the Egyptian gods. He'd survived the Passover with the blood of an innocent lamb on his door. He'd been led into the desert by pillars of cloud and fire. He'd seen the parting of the Red Sea and passed safely through watery walls on dry ground. He'd witnessed the sudden destruction of the earth's most powerful army by God's hand.

He'd watched bitter waters made pure, manna appear on the ground, quail in the desert, and water gush from a rock. He'd come to Mount Sinai *"that burned with fire, and to blackness and darkness and tempest, and the sound of a trumpet and the voice of words, so that those who heard it begged that the word should not be spoken to them anymore"* (Hebrews 12:18–19 NKJV). He'd ascended this mountain not once but twice, fasting forty days in God's presence. He'd received the stone tablets written by God's finger and received the revelation of God's tabernacle, a foreshadowing of things to come.

He'd met face to face with God, who knew him by name; he'd found grace in His sight. Yet after all Moses had seen and experienced, he'd only seen the residue of God's glory. Now he wanted more!

BEYOND SIGNS AND WONDERS

What does this teach us? That the glory of God is beyond signs and wonders. God's works reflect His glory, but God's glory is His character.

His works reflect His character: He is good, gracious, compassionate, and holy. Yet He will by no means leave the guilty unpunished. No man can look on His face and live. Only one place is safe enough to allow God's glory to draw near: "in the cleft of the Rock" covered by His hand. Only from that place can we bear to gaze upon the holy character of an eternal God. And that Rock, which followed the Israelites in the desert and which shelters us from the wrath of a just and loving God, is Christ. To see God's glory we must hide ourselves in Jesus. Only in Him can we bear to hear and see the proclamation of the Father's glory.

The Lord, the Lord God, merciful and gracious, longsuffering, and abounding in goodness and truth, keeping mercy for thousands, forgiving iniquity and transgression and sin, by no means clearing the guilty, visiting the iniquity of the father upon the children and the children's children to the third and the fourth generation. (Exodus 34:6–7 NKJV)

As we draw near to Christ, we draw near to God's glory. But do we grow so satisfied with "the God of signs and wonders" that we stop seeking Him as a Person? Do we presume to draw near to Him without reverence for His holiness and power? Do we fail to hide ourselves in the cleft of the Rock? Perhaps this is why God, in His mercy, refuses to draw near.

Moses had seen more than any of us will ever see in a lifetime, and he learned something most of us have yet to realize. God is holy, God is a person, and His glory far exceeds mere miracles. Let us hunger and pray for God's glory as Moses did. If we see what Moses saw, we'll get what Moses got, and it will forever change our lives and the lives of those for whom we pray.

Once again, God's glory is neither His power nor His presence. *God's glory is His character.* When we understand His character, we see His glory. When we see His glory, we understand His character. Why do people weep in the Lord's presence? Not because they sense His presence but because they sense the character within that presence. Why do people tremble in fear when they see God's power? Not because they feel His power but because they feel the character that wields that power.

After God revealed His glory to Moses, Scripture records no rebellion until after Moses' death. God's glory changed one man, and the residue of that glory, clinging to that one man, changed a whole generation. Isn't that what we're called to do—represent God's glory to all creation? Will the glory clinging to us change our generation? Is our goal truly that "the earth will be filled with the knowledge of the glory of the Lord, as the waters cover the sea" (Habakkuk 2:14 NKJV)? Then let's pray that we will be prepared to behold God's glory and that, through us, God will reveal His glory to all people as we preach the gospel of Jesus Christ.

THE GLORY CLOUD

The cloud was *not* the glory; it *contained* the glory! God is a consuming fire (Hebrews 12:29), and the cloud hides us from the consuming intensity and absolute purity of His holy love. The countenance of that love is Jesus Christ (John 3:16). He is the radiance of the Father's glory and the exact representation of His nature (Hebrews 1:3). His eyes are a flame of fire (Revelation 19:12). His feet are like burnished bronze (2:18) glowing in the furnace. His face is like the sun shining in its strength (1:14–16). He is the Bright Morning Star (22:16).

The people who walk in darkness will see a great light (Isaiah 9:2), a light of revelation to the Gentiles (Luke 2:32). Jesus is the light of the world (John 8:12), the light that blinded Paul on the road to Damascus (Acts 9:3). He is the one who will baptize us with the Holy Spirit and fire (Matthew 3:11). He was in the pillars of cloud and fire that led Israel by day and by night (Exodus 13:21). He's the one who came to Moses in the thick cloud, with thunder, lightning flashes, and trumpet sound, with fire and smoke that ascended as from a furnace and that caused the whole mountain to quake violently when Moses received the Law (19:18–20; 20:18–20). It was the residue of *His* glory that shone on Moses' face.

Jesus is the glory of the cloud that descended in the tabernacle (40:34–35), in the temple (2 Chronicles 5:13–14), and in the cloud that appeared above the ark of the covenant (Leviticus 16:2). He is the character of God revealed to man (Exodus 34). He is the terrible fire of judgment that consumed those who offered unauthorized fire in the tabernacle of the Lord (Leviticus 10:2), that consumed the offering of Elijah on Mount Carmel (1 Kings 18:38), and that consumed a captain and his fifty men who conspired against Elijah (2 Kings 1:10–12).

Christ is the light of the rainbow of God's covenant promise (Genesis 8). He is the one whose appearance in the furnace, heated seven times over, shown "like a son of the gods" and protected His innocent worshipers from even the smell of smoke (Daniel 3:25–27). The sun dims in comparison to His glory. He is the Rock, the Lamb, the Fire, and the Altar. He is the Sacrifice. He is the Lord.

The light of the knowledge of God's glory can be seen in Christ's face (2 Corinthians 4:6). He is the lamp of the New Jerusalem (Revelation 21:23). Jesus is the glory of God incarnate!

> *And the city has no need of the sun or of the moon to shine upon it, for the glory of God has illumined it, and its lamp is the Lamb.* (Revelation 21:23)

> *God, who at various times and in various ways spoke in time past to the fathers by the prophets, has in these last days spoken to us by His Son, whom He has appointed heir of all things, through whom also he made the worlds; who being* the brightness of His glory *and the express image of His person, and upholding all things by the word of His power, when He had by Himself purged our sins, sat down at the right hand of the Majesty on high, having become so much better than the angels, as He has by inheritance obtained a more excellent name than they.* (Hebrews 1:1–4 NKJV)

CLOTHED IN CHRIST

It's time for us to clothe ourselves in Christ and bring Him the glory due His name. It is time "to win for the Lamb the reward of His suffering" (motto of the Moravian Brethren). In Christ we are living threads, strands of light, woven together as a garment of praise unto the Lord. We were designed to reflect a measure of His glory. If we fail to live according to His design, He'll not receive the glory we were designed to reflect. There is a glory realm called heaven, where He receives all the glory due His name. But the earth is presently under Satan's dominion, and to the degree that we do not live according to God's design, to that degree He does not receive the glory that is His just and right due.

If we'll walk by faith, we cannot lose. If we pray in faith to raise the dead and the dead *are* raised, the gospel is preached, souls are saved, and God is glorified. If we pray in faith to raise the dead and the dead are *not* raised, the major obstacle to the preaching of the gospel (our carnal nature and our fear of man) is crucified, the gospel is preached, souls are saved, and God is glorified. Either way, when we walk by faith in obedience we win. As true Christians, the only way we can ever lose is by doing nothing at all. "All that is necessary for the triumph of evil is that good men do nothing" (Edmund Burke).

The day will come when God's children, His servants, will live fully according to His design. In that day, the earth *will* be full of the knowledge of His glory as the waters cover the sea. Let's hasten the day of His coming glory by wrapping ourselves in the character of Christ and allowing ourselves to be woven together into a garment of praise worthy of His name.

KEY POINTS

(1) The glory of God is far above signs, wonders, and mere miracles.

(2) God's works reflect His glory, but God's glory is His character.

(3) As we draw near to Christ, we draw near to God's glory.

(4) It's because we fail to hide ourselves in the cleft of the Rock that God, in His mercy, refuses to draw near.

(5) The residue of God's glory, clinging to one man, can change a generation.

(6) The glory is *not* the cloud. The glory is *in* the cloud to shield us from the consuming intensity and absolute purity of God's holy love.

(7) Jesus is the glory of God incarnate!

(8) In Christ alone, God receives the full measure of glory He designed man to reflect.

SPIRITUAL RECONNAISSANCE

(1) Has God's glory ever invaded our church or region and brought with it a spirit of repentance and weeping?

(2) What key experiences have formed the corporate relationship of our congregation with God, and what did we learn about God from them?

(3) To what characteristics of God has the attention of our church or community been directed as we observed the signs and wonders performed in our midst?

(4) Does a residue of that revelation of God's character remain imprinted on the collective memory of our church?

(5) What are we doing to preserve or obscure that revelation?

(6) What are we doing to magnify that revelation in our community?

(7) As a church, does our relationship to the community reflect that we are clothed in Christ?

(8) As a church, is our faith in God sufficiently evident to adequately reflect His glory to the community?

PERSONALIZE IT

(1) Has God's glory ever invaded my life or home and brought with it a spirit of repentance and weeping?

(2) What key experiences have formed the corporate relationship of my family with God, and what did I learn about God from them?

(3) To what characteristics of God has my attention been directed as I observed the signs and wonders performed in my midst?

(4) Does a residue of that revelation of God's character remain

imprinted on my memory and on the collective memory of my family?

(5) What am I doing to preserve or obscure that revelation?

(6) What am I doing to magnify that revelation in my life and family?

(7) Does my relationship to others (saved and pre-saved) reflect that I am clothed in Christ?

(8) Is my faith in God sufficiently evident to reflect His glory to others?